Responsible
Sexuality –
NOW

Responsible
Sexuality–
NOW

BY
DEANE
WILLIAM
FERM

The Seabury Press

NEW YORK

To my wife
PAULIE
and our four children
BILL
LIN
BOB
LAURIE

Ett gott skratt
förlänger livit!

PREFACE

During the academic year 1965–66 my family and I lived in Sweden, where I studied the relationship between the churches of Sweden and the social problems of contemporary Swedish society. I returned to Sweden during the fall of 1969 to attend the First International Symposium on Sexology. One fact that has become increasingly clear to me is that the most obvious reason why the churches in Sweden have been so ineffective in the contemporary social scene is their resistance to social change, and more specifically for our interest, their refusal to develop a modern, creative, and positive approach to the role of sex. Although the churches in the United States are presently more vigorous and healthy than the churches of Sweden, still they are playing a diminishing role in influencing American social policies. I am convinced that their only hope for staying alive is to "get with it" and tackle this problem of human sexuality with no holds barred.

To quote Professor J. C. Wynn of Colgate-Rochester Divinity School: "The time has come when Christians will have to acknowledge the undeniable existence of sex. Then perhaps we can build on our feeble beginnings of educating our church members for this important area of living." This is not an easy task since many church people have more hang-ups about sex than they do about war and racism. As one ex-nun said recently: "Why is the Church so overboard on sex instead of the nuclear bomb, war, and the conditions of the poor?"

But the stakes are too high to dodge the issue. To refuse to respond courageously and affirmatively is not only to rot, but also a frank admission that we do not recognize how serious are the social problems related to sex. The churches also must recognize that we now live in a pluralistic society, and we must be willing to tolerate forms of sexual behavior that go against our own personal preferences. This is the price that we have to pay for living in a democratic society, but it is a price worth paying. I see the crucial role of the church today as that of creating a norm for human sexuality that will go beyond her own members and encompass all citizens who wish to enhance the dignity of man and the dimension of love in all human relationships. If she speaks only to herself, then she will remain outside the action which, by the way, is what has happened to the churches in Sweden. I am more concerned to have the churches speak to all America than primarily to the chosen few.

One final personal note. Some readers may think that I am just another college chaplain trying to be "relevant." I wish to report that my wife and I have four wonderful teen-age children, and if they choose to follow the ideas that I suggest in this book, I would be most pleased.

Readers of my articles, which appeared in *The American Scandinavian Review* (1967), *Christian Century* (1966, 1970), *Mount Holyoke Alumnae Quarterly,* and *Religious Education* (1969), will recognize the use here of some ideas previously expressed in those journals.

I wish to express my indebtedness to the following individuals for their helpful suggestions derived from their reading all or sections of this manuscript: my former teacher at Yale University Divinity School, Professor Roland Bainton; my colleagues at Mount Holyoke College, Professors John Lobb and Charles Trout; my good friend Rabbi Solomon Kaplan of Congregation Sons of Zion in Pittsburgh, Pa.; my former student Mrs. Patricia Roth Schwartz; and my Swedish expert Mrs. Elisabeth Wettergren. I am grateful to Arthur Buckley of Seabury Press for his sound advice and constant encouragement; to the Faculty Grants Committee of Mount Holyoke College, who made it possible for me to attend the Swedish Symposium on Sexology; and to my loyal secretary, Mrs. Mildred March, who not only typed the manuscript but also helped to eliminate grammatical errors, including a few dangling participles. Most of all I thank my wife and four children, who, by their love and loyalty, have convinced me of the truth of Martin Buber's conviction that "all real living is meeting."

DEANE WILLIAM FERM

Payment Lake
Mercer, Wisconsin
July 1970.

CONTENTS

Three

Four

INTRODUCTION

We are living in a time of rapid social change which has radically challenged age-old attitudes toward sex, marriage, and the family. Fewer and fewer Americans seem to believe that sex is essentially for procreation, marriage is for life, and the family consists of father as breadwinner, mother as housekeeper, and children as loyal followers of parental authority. These values, so long an essential ingredient of Western tradition and our Christian civilization, are not live options for increasing numbers of our citizens.

Even more unsettling are the pervasive social problems which make the present challenge so critical and solutions so imperative. Here are a few disturbing trends:

1. Since World War II a lax attitude toward sexual encounters, especially among the young, has been increasing steadily. Although some observers argue that this tolerant approach has not led to more permissive sexual experience, recent studies suggest that behavior is now catching up with the new ideas. A Gallup Poll of fifty-five campuses indicated that 75 percent of the students interviewed believed that it was no longer im-

portant that the person they marry be a virgin—an opinion voiced by about an equal proportion of men and women.[1] A study instituted by the Institute for Sex Research at Indiana University revealed that college girls have far less guilt feelings toward premarital sex than their counterparts of twenty years ago.[2] A professor at Brown University has said that "the adolescent subculture is moving toward a no-rule situation" in sex. A study at Oberlin College in Ohio in 1969 shows a significant increase in sexual activity among students over even the previous year. The 1968 poll indicated that 39.6 percent of women students had had intercourse that year; in 1969, the percentage had risen to 48.7 percent, larger even than for the men students. Also, a study of Oberlin college seniors showed that 71.8 percent of the women and 65.6 percent of the men had had previous sexual relations.[3] These figures point not only to a dramatic increase in permissive sexual behavior but also to an end to the double standard that has long been tacitly accepted.

2. From 1964 to 1966, one-third of all first-born children in the United States were conceived out of wedlock. Many marriages were hastily arranged to give the babies legitimacy, but even then one out of seven was born illegitimate. Forty-two percent of women under age twenty had their first-born before they had been married eight months; the highest proportion of these young mothers had had one to three years of high school.[4]

3. The venereal disease rate is rising dramatically. Venereal disease is second only to the common cold as the nation's most common communicable disease. There is now a nation-wide epidemic of gonorrhea. The reported incidence of gonorrhea has risen 15 percent in the past year, more than 200 percent in some of the larger cities, and in high schools in these urban areas, a student has one in five chances of getting VD before graduation. Statistically a teenager gets VD every two minutes somewhere in the United States, and this does not

include all the cases that go unreported. Although private physicians treat about 80 percent of the cases, they report only about one in nine to public health officials.[5]

4. In the United States annually there are between 500,000 and 1,500,000 abortions. Illegal abortions occur at the rate of about one out of five children conceived. About 10 to 20 percent of women who have illegal abortions experience complications following the operation. Approximately one million actual births annually are unwanted.[6]

5. Living together without benefit of legal marriage has become increasingly popular in the larger urban areas, where it is relatively simple to live anonymously and even clandestinely as far as the folks back home are concerned. The liaison is often without commitment or any intention of permanence. Some individuals are urging either the abolition of marriage or, failing that, "probationary marriage" for a trial period. Children of this kind of arrangement are, under the present laws, often orphaned or at least left without adequate care and protection. A psychiatrist at the University of California in Berkeley said recently, "Stable, open, nonmarital relationships are pushing the border of what society is going to face in ten years."

6. In the past forty years the divorce rate has tripled. Although the rate has remained fairly steady for the last few years, it is now beginning to rise again. Presently about one in every three and a half marriages ends in divorce, and in California, the percentage is even higher—one out of two marriages do not last. If to the figure of divorce, that of desertion (poor man's divorce) is added, the total is truly alarming.

7. An increasing number of American women are now working outside the home. The percentage of women who remain home to keep house has dropped to 48.4 percent, compared with 57 percent in 1957. The largest increase in women who work has been among married women with children, yet women continue to be discriminated against in terms

of job preference and salary. The occupations employing the largest number of women—teaching, nursing, cooking, cleaning, and making clothes—are functions that have moved from home to some institution. In 1957 women engaged in full-time employment earned a median wage of $3,008 a year; the median wage of men was $4,713. By 1968 women's median income had increased by 51 percent to $4,550, while men's salary had gone up 65 percent to $7,800. Clearly this sex discrimination cannot be defended much longer on moral or legal grounds. Moreover, this increasing desire on the part of mothers to work outside the home—however desirable it may be—does raise serious questions about the traditional structure of the family.

8. Added to these particular social problems is the critical world population explosion. The world's population is presently about 3.5 billion, more than double the figure of 1900. With the present rate of increase, there will be 7 billion people by the year 2000. Half of the population today has been born since the end of World War II. Currently the world's population is getting an average of about 2,000 calories per day. By the year 2000, this will drop to an average of 1,340, below what experts have estimated is the "absolute starvation level" of 1,350 calories a day. We may soon see the day when the birth of a child anywhere in the world will seem more of a curse than a blessing.

What do we do about these present-day facts of life? Do we try to ignore them and hope somehow the bad will go away? Do we continue to preach the same moral and religious platitudes that have been proclaimed for centuries, and then blame the people for not accepting our advice? Or do we search for a new meaning to sexuality that will both honor the dignity and worth of genuine human relationships and be applicable to our period of history?

This book is an attempt to take the last alternative seriously. Fortunately the general public now is coming to realize the serious nature of our social problems and the need for public debate about what should be done to solve them. I hope that I can contribute to that debate. I have three objectives in mind. First, I want to show that our dominant Christian, Western, and American attitude toward sex, marriage, and the family has been largely negative and unhealthy and is in some respects doing more harm than good. Second, I believe that Sweden has confronted social change in the twentieth century realistically and positively. She has developed models for human relationships and the meaning of sexuality which the United States would do well to examine. Indeed, it is my conviction that we are moving rapidly in the direction of the Swedish sexual morality whether we like it or not. Therefore, we should learn from the Swedish way—both the positive and negative factors. Third, I want to suggest the meaning of responsible sexuality for our day and the implications thereof for our country and our churches.

One

A LOOK
AT THE PAST

Man is apparently the only living animal who has developed guilt feelings about his sexual desires. Nothing innate about him has yet been discovered to explain this guilt. His attitude toward sex, marriage and the family is a culmination of developing cultural and social expectations that "worked" for a particular group of people—expectations which were eventually given privileged status by society and religion. There is scarcely any manifestation of sexual behavior that has not been approved and forbidden at one time or another. The fate of history could possibly have made contemporary sexual norms turn out differently. Although certain norms have been dominant throughout history, they are by no means exclusive of other types.

EARLY MAN

We do not really know the sexual customs and practices of early man. We can only infer certain data from a study of similar simple societies that are in existence today. Apparently no one pattern of sexual behavior gained total acceptance among early man and his tribes. The wandering nomads treated sex as a normal bodily function. Indeed conception was often not connected with intercourse, but was thought to be caused by the moon, by being present in certain sacred places or even by eating particular foods. Sex habits depended on the local situation and the preferences of the group. It is impossible to take a mass of varying practices and come up with an hypothesis as to the attitude of early man to sex, marriage, and the family.

Yet certain mores did eventually develop which, although not universal, gradually won widespread approval. Most important was that the male was considered the superior sex. He was thought to be more intelligent and stronger, and consequently took the major share of responsibility for manual labor. But this male superiority was not universally true as Margaret Mead and other anthropologists have reminded us. It was woman's biological fate to bear the children, and this fact limited her physical capacity. It also gave her prime responsibility for caring for her offspring. Since the mother gave birth to the children, her role was akin to that of nature. She begat the human race in the same way that Mother Nature produced all living things. For this reason early deities were often female, although this honor had no effect on mortal woman's inferior status.

Some arrangement was needed to allow for the procreation of children and for their care until old enough to take care of themselves. We can define the institution of marriage as a more or less stable union between a man and a woman (or men and women), which normally continued until after the birth and early years of the children. Although some scholars trace the origin of marriage to the mating habits of animals, marriage between humans also included certain social sanctions. It was a means of controlling the relationship between the sexes and of supervising the rearing of small children.

The need to care for offspring was for early man the primary reason for the institution of the family. Love or romance need play no part in this arrangement. The family unit was virtually universal among early tribes. This unit was the progenitor of the conjugal or nuclear family, consisting of the married man and woman and their children, related by marriage, blood, or adoption and generally living together under one roof. The members of this loosely structured group developed common traditions and mores. Their roles to each other depended on their particular function, for example, father, sister, son, etc. The essential element in family life, past and present, is the subordination of the interests and values of the individual to the larger concerns of the group. From earliest times the family not only protected the young until they could manage for themselves, but also fulfilled the human need to belong and to be accepted by a small group. Marriage and the family to early man were relations of convenience and not covenants for happiness.

As time passed, new economic organizations developed. The growth of agriculture and the domestication of animals gave stability to the supply of food and made hunting forays less frequent. The father developed an attachment both to the land and to the clan. The longer he remained home, the more he established his superior role. His alleged male superiority caused him to dominate his wife and his children. One of the earliest widespread practices coming from this assumed privileged status was the belief that the man could, by some form of payment, secure property rights to a woman. Since early times women's rights have been a form of property rights. The man would literally give property in exchange for property. Later this belief was expressed in the concept of the dowry the daughter brought to her new household. The dowry was paid by the father of the bride to the groom. It was a bond for holding the marriage together. Even today the notion that the woman should be a virgin before marriage is a remnant of the belief that the man has claims on his wife that no other man has, the right to private and pure property.

Normally marriage and sexual relationships between parent and sibling came to be prohibited although in some tribes they were permitted between brother and sister. At times group marriages were practiced, but jealousy and insecurity usually made such arrangements unsatisfactory. Some people encouraged marriage outside the family or clan (exogamy), while others encouraged it within certain specific groups (endogamy). The most common form of marriage was a loosely structured monogamy, or less often polygyny (the union of one husband and two or more wives). Polyandry (the union of one wife and several husbands) was far less common. Polygyny was most popular among the wealthy or those higher in status since only they could afford the added economic and social burdens. However, modified monogamy became most prevalent because it seemed to have the fewest problems. Most societies had a relatively equal number of men and women. Monogamy was an efficient unit in the struggle for survival, gave a sense of stability and acceptance to small children, and prevented the jealousies which can become so intense when a person believes that someone else is using "property" which he insists belongs to him. Monogamy as the dominant form of marriage was due to a combination of social and economic circumstances which later became imbedded in tradition and still later was given religious sanction.

In subsequent centuries in most parts of the Western world, marriage took on greater importance, not only for reasons of convenience, but also because it insured the continuation of the family. Marriage became a means of uniting the family to common ancestors. Kinship groups thus broadened the monogamous pattern and gave it historical perspective. Some tribes traced their lineage through the mother (matrilineal) and others through the father (patrilineal). Matronymic descent was common in Asia and some sections of early America. Patrilineal descent was the practice in China, Rome, Israel, and most primitive societies. Yet even in the matrilineal societies, where women conferred status, men held the dominant power.

A woman at marriage usually became a member of her husband's family, taking up his customs and following his gods. Early marriage was encouraged as a means for insuring a partner. It was a contractual arrangement between families and not individuals. However, if the husband tired of his wife, he could divorce her by paying back his original purchase price. Divorce was strictly a private bargain for the men. Only a very few tribes did not permit this procedure for divorce. Adultery was condemned since it was a usurpation of the property rights of another man. Adultery was also an intrusion into the family unit. An adult who remained unmarried was blamed for not fulfilling his social responsibilities to his family and to his ancestors, a view which has persisted in many societies including the United States to this day. The attitude toward premarital sex varied from tribe to tribe. Some encouraged free sexual relationships, with greater laxity given to the boys. Other tribes strictly regulated the sexual function. In these latter tribes the unmarried woman was expected to remain chaste unless her father or the chieftain could find some use for her that might favor the father or the tribe. In some early societies the single woman was offered by her owner, the father, as a prostitute for his financial gain.

Woman's two primary assets were the begetting of children and her economic value. She took care of the home and often produced goods in the home. The children were treated as wards of the parents. The boys began at a tender age to work for their fathers, and the girls served their mothers as helpers. The mortality rate was astoundingly high. Abortions and infanticide (especially for girls) were not uncommon, usually for economic reasons. To be sure, the killing of female infants became a practice only in those societies where girls were a liability, i.e., where dowries had to be paid. The harshness of life and scarcity of food dictated many offspring but few survivors.

In short, the early family was an economic and social arrangement which provided some stability for its members and a nest for the fledglings. It was a part of a larger family, the tribe, which tended to regulate marriage and sexual patterns for the sake of some sense of shared values. This larger family supervised mores and education and sought to pass on its customs to the young. In a very real sense the tribe of primitive societies served the same function as the schools and churches of today. Since sexual practices are shaped by cultural factors, these norms sometimes are foreign to biological needs. Individual sexual desires, unplanned pregnancies, and adultery created problems for early man as they still do today. Shared values may be necessary to provide stability for a society, but oftentimes the tensions that they create are destructive for some members of that society.

THE CLASSICAL PERIOD

As major social and economic changes began to take place in the Western world in the centuries preceding the Christian era, marriage customs were challenged. We have noted how marriage as a relationship of convenience was later reinforced by the sanctions of society and religion. This view began to give way under Roman influence to the notion that marriage was a private matter between man and woman which could be made and broken at will. Among the wealthy the exchange of property at marriage became less important. Although the husband remained the head of the house, the wife often received financial assistance from her father. She used her money as a bribe to demand more independence from her spouse. This increasing freedom threatened the structure of marriage. Divorce became more prevalent, with the exchange of property less crucial for people of means. Indeed, it was this breakdown of marriage and family life which in part led the early Christians to attack Roman practices and their gods. The Christian critique was also directed against the variety of sexual unions that were being formed outside of the marital relationship.

The survival of marriage became a matter of increasing importance to the Roman authorities who feared a breakdown of all institutions including the government. After all, what was the point of marriage if there was no economic need and if sexual desire could be fulfilled in other ways? Consequently, the birth rate fell, prostitution increased, and infanticide and abortion became common practice. Even the poor abandoned the newborn. What, then, would happen to the propagation of the race? One Roman official, writing in the second century B.C., declared: "If we could live without wives, we should be rid of that nuisance; but since nature has decreed that we can neither live comfortably with them nor live at all without them, we must e'en look rather to our permanent interests than to a passing pleasure." [1]

The Emperor Caesar Augustus became so concerned about the elimination of marriage and children that he passed a law, A.D. 9, that bachelors between 25 and 60 and spinsters between 20 and 50 were not allowed to inherit property unless they married within one hundred days. He offered rewards for large families. When adultery became widespread, an Adultery Law took from the husband the right to kill his wife if he caught her being unfaithful, although her partner in crime could still be murdered. The unfaithful wife lost half her money and was banished to a desolate island. One of the first to pay this penalty was Julia, the daughter of Augustus, who was banished to the island of Pandatoria, where she supposedly died of starvation.

The institution of marriage also suffered in the Greek tradition, and the role of woman was even more miserable. The wife was confined to the home where she belonged, not to be seen by others. An Athenian woman had no status in court; she was the silent and private property of her husband. With wives safely hidden in the home, men went out to seek their pleasure. "The best woman," said Pericles, "is she of whom men speak the least." Prostitution increased. In the centuries immediately preceding the Christian era a special type of woman called the "hataera" came to prominence. They lived independently, were full of charm and sex appeal, and sold their wares to eager men. They were the "kept women" of wealthy society, far higher in status than the prostitutes. Their role as mistresses was aptly described by Demosthenes: "Mistresses we keep for pleasure, concubines for daily attendance upon our persons, and wives to bear us legitimate children and be our housekeepers." [2]

Little wonder, then, that marriage was downgraded. As the Greek poet Palladas put it: "Marriage brings a man only two happy days: the day he takes his bride to bed, and the day he lays her in her grave." [3]

Some Greek men took a greater interest in young boys, a form of affection known as pederasty. In a society where all images of perfection and beauty were anthropoid, the young boy most nearly approximated the ideal. With a boy a man could enjoy himself without danger of permanent entanglement or the begetting of children.

To be sure, most of these changes in Roman and Greek society affected only the wealthier classes. The lower economic classes retained the patriarchal system with the women and children as chattel of the father. But sexual permissiveness among the poor did increase as did divorce and the abandonment of small children. In virtually every case the advantage was all the man's. The value of the patriarchal family, then as now, was its stabilizing factor for society. It did maintain a sense of security and belonging which every society needs in order to survive. When marriage and the family break down, so does society.

THE OLD TESTAMENT

The early Christian attitude toward sex and marriage was in large part a reaction to the increasing laxity of Greco-Roman society. But it was also a fulfillment of some basic Jewish attitudes and in part an opposition to certain legalistic practices that had developed in later Judaism. Early Israel's neighbors had developed sexual behavior patterns quite different from her own. These neighbors had centered their religion in nature and the cycle of seasons. In Egypt this emphasis on Mother Nature led to the emergence of a matriarchy. Women owned property, and inheritances were usually through the mother's lineage. Women as well as men could divorce and remarry. Often the Pharaoh would marry his sister in order to preserve the purity of his lineage. As other cultures became assimilated into Egypt's, patriarchy became the rule. Divorce became rare, and prostitution was regularly practiced.

The religion of Babylon was rampant with temple prostitution, which was true among most of the nature cults. Premarital sexual relations were permitted, but marital fidelity, especially for the woman, was expected. Marriages were usually arranged by the parents. The woman was not permitted to divorce, but the man could get rid of his wife by returning her dowry. The code of Hammurabi gave certain rights to women, particularly part of the dowry and the father's estate. If a husband left his wife for a long period of time, his wife was permitted to have relations with another man without breaking up the original marriage. Assyria likewise had a nature religion, but from the outset Assyria was more patriarchal in character. Men had concubines, and the state officially sanctioned prostitution. The Canaanites were similar to the Assyrians, with their religion imbedded in nature and fertility rites, and their gods participating in their sexual practices.

The Hebrews opposed the excessive sexuality of the fertility cults. They did not give sexual attributes to Yahweh nor expect him to participate fully in sexual rites. For them sex was good if used properly, for it was a dimension of God's creation. For the Hebrews man was a unity of body and soul. Sex was neither idolized nor minimized, but considered a normal and natural function of man's total being. Celibacy was not encouraged, and eunuchs were excluded from the congregation (Deuteronomy 3:1). The barrenness of a wife was grounds for divorce.

Hebraic society was strictly patriarchal in character. Eve was created out of Adam's rib. God expected woman to be subservient to man: "To the woman he said, 'I will greatly multiply your pain in childbearing; in pain shall you bring forth children, yet your desire shall be for your husband, and he shall rule over you'" (Genesis 3:16).

The covenant decalogue listed his wife among a man's possessions (Exodus 20:17). Baal was a term that designated both the God of the tribe and the father of the household. When a woman married, she became a part of her husband's family. The role of the Jewish wife was well summarized by the Rabbi who remarked: "When the husband occupies a chair in Paradise, his wife is his footstool." [4] Sarah was the ideal Jewess because she was a support to her husband and a champion of her children. The husband could divorce his wife at will (Deuteronomy 24:1), but a wife could not divorce her husband. Later the school of Shammai allowed a husband to get a divorce only for adultery or misbehavior. The more liberal school of Hillel was more permissive in granting divorces. The Hillel attitude prevailed and is the standard used today. Even now, according to traditional Judaism, only the husband may institute divorce proceedings.

Adultery for man or woman was not tolerated (Exodus 20:14). If a woman was believed to be unfaithful to her husband, he could take her to the priest who would make her drink of the water of bitterness. If she was innocent, she was freed and could conceive children. If she was guilty, then "may this water that brings the curse pass into your bowels and make your body swell and your thighs fall away" (Numbers 5:22).

Sodomy, which included both sexual relations with persons of the same sex and with animals, was forbidden. Indeed the term *sodomy* comes from the men of Sodom, who supposedly practiced homosexuality (Genesis 19:5). Another passage is explicit in its condemnation of sodomy: "You shall not lie with a male as with a woman; it is an abomination. And you shall not lie with any beast and defile yourself with it, neither shall any woman give herself to a beast to lie with it: It is perversion" (Leviticus 18:22–23).

The role of the woman was to marry, bear children and care for the family. Women were not considered as full persons as is indicated in this passage: "Jeremiah said to all the people *and all the women* . . ." (Jeremiah 44:24). If her husband died with her still childless, the deceased man's closest male relative was to marry her and beget an offspring, a custom known as the *levirate*. The levirate marriage started out as a tribal device and eventually became an economic factor tied in with maintaining the property within tribal boundaries. A ceremony of release was and still is possible. Polygyny was lawful as it was a means of begetting more offspring, the limitations being the practical ones of the supply of women, the financial resources, and man's ability to meet the sexual needs of his wives. The interpretation in the Mishnah of Exodus 21:10, where a husband may not favor one wife over the other, is interpreted in Ketuboth verses 6 and 7 to refer not only to the economic needs but to the sexual ones as well. A large number of the ancient Hebrews married two wives. After the Babylonian Exile in the sixth century B.C., monogamy became the established pattern. Polygyny has been practiced in Moslem countries until the present day, and many Yemenite Jews, in recent years, have come to Israel with two or more wives.

Other customs developed concerning children, betrothal, and marriage. The Hebrews required a double period of purification after the birth of a girl. If a child struck or cursed either parent, he was to be put to death (Exodus 21:15, 17). However, this law was apparently never applied. A father could sell his children to save himself from bankruptcy, and sell his daughter to pay off debts. If an unmarried woman had sexual relations, ordinarily the only disability that she suffered was that when she was ready to marry, she would not receive the dowry of a virgin. If she was seduced by a man who wanted to marry her, then marriage was the punishment! There was no law concerning sexual relations between couples planning to marry as long as no child was conceived; conception simply meant an earlier marriage. A relationship with an unmarried female, while not applauded, was certainly not considered adultery unless she was betrothed to another man, in which case she would be considered married. Marriage was an agreement between the fathers; no civil or religious ceremony was expected. Although there are examples in the Old Testament of love between husband and wife, still love was not the reason for marriage. The Song of Solomon is a collection of sensual love poems some of which may have originally been sung at weddings, but most of which were probably songs between lovers. For example:

> Behold, you are beautiful, my love,
> Behold, you are beautiful! . . .
> Your lips are like a scarlet thread,
> And your mouth is lovely. . . .
> You have ravished my heart, my sister, my bride.

You have ravished my heart with a glance of your eyes,
With one jewel of your necklace,
How sweet is your love, my sister, my bride!
SONG OF SOLOMON 4:1, 3, 9–10

But such a feeling of romance was not regarded as necessary or even desirable in a marriage relationship. It was a man's world, and however he might appreciate and even on occasion love his wife, he was in command, and she held an inferior place:

A good wife who can find?
She is far more precious than jewels.
The heart of her husband trusts in her,
And he will have no lack of gain.
She does him good, and not harm,
all the days of her life.
She seeks wool and flax,
and works with willing hands.
She is like the ships of the merchant,
She brings her food from afar.
She rises while it is yet night
And provides food for her household
And tasks for her maidens.
PROVERBS 31:10–16

Good wives were hard to find, but no matter how good they were, their role was to provide for the household and serve their husbands. Their place was not with their husbands sitting among the elders of the land, but seeking wool and flax and working with willing hands in the home. If and only if they did these things, would their husbands rise up and praise them. The King's daughter is all glorious within the palace (Psalms 45:14), but not outside of it. While Hebrew women were far from equal to men, their status among the ancient Israelites was still higher than it was among the surrounding peoples.

THE NEW TESTAMENT

The New Testament is a fulfillment of the Old Testament, from the Christian point of view, and follows the basic teaching of Judaism, more specifically Palestinian Judaism. However, the situation in the first century of the Christian era was marked by Greco-Roman immorality and Jewish legalism. The early Christians sought to keep a balance between these two opposite forces of permissiveness and rigidity.

Jesus apparently made no antifeminist statements as such. He treated women as persons and often singled out women condemned by society to show the meaning of his message of love and forgiveness. Christianity was for both men and women, and their spiritual plane was equal. Yet Jesus followed the prevailing attitude in debasing woman at the same time that he prized her. There were no women among the twelve disciples nor the seventy elders. The Lord's Supper was instituted in the presence of men only. The apostolic commissions (John 20:19–23; Matthew 28:16–20) were for men only, and no woman authored a New Testament book. It is significant that Jesus ministered for the most part to men, yet women ministered to him. His stress was on the domestic responsibilities of women. The chief missionaries were men, and the leadership of the church was in the hands of men.

As we have noted, Jewish law allowed for divorce. Jesus, however, was against divorce (Mark 10:11–12) except possibly in the case of adultery: "And I say to you: whoever divorces his wife, except for unchastity, and marries another, commits adultery" (Matthew 19:9). Jesus' emphasis was on inner motivation, which determined the outward acts: "But I say to you that everyone who looks at a woman lustfully has already committed adultery with her in his heart" (Matthew 5:27). Jesus was not so much repealing the Jewish law that permitted divorce as he was saying what ideally should be experienced in a marriage.

The Apostle Paul developed more explicit views concerning sexuality and marriage, views which were to become dominant in the early Christian Church. Paul viewed the pagan world as filled with homosexuality, prostitution, and all manner of sexual promiscuity. He considered this the result of pagan idolatry, and because these pagans refused to honor the true God, "God gave them up in the lusts of their hearts to impurity, to the dishonoring of their bodies among themselves, because they exchanged the truth about God for a lie and worshipped and served the creature rather than the Creator" (Romans 1:24–25).

Paul preferred that all men remain single like himself (I Corinthians 7:7) because of the imminent second coming of Christ. Yet if this was not possible and because of the temptation to immorality, "each man should have his own wife and each wife her own husband" (I Corinthians 7:2). Married couples should not abstain from sex for too long since this might tempt them to immorality. The important point is that "it is better to marry than be aflame with passion" (I Corinthians 7:9). Marriage was to be monogamous and for life (Romans 7:2,3). A second marriage was possible only if the first partner was deceased. Marriage to a non-Christian was not grounds for divorce unless the unbelieving partner wished to separate. Children born into Christian homes, even if only one of the parents was a Christian, were still considered of the faith.

The role of the woman was to glorify Christ in her relationship to her husband: "Woman is the glory of man. For man was not made from woman, but woman from man" (I Corinthians 11:7–8). "Wives, be subject to your husbands, as to the Lord. For the husband is the head of the wife as Christ is head of the church . . . let wives be subject in everything to their husbands . . ." (Ephesians 5:22,24).

The woman was inferior to the man in her marital relationship and in her place in the church as well: "As in all the churches of the saints, the women should keep silence in the churches. For they are not permitted to speak, but should be subordinate, as even the law says. If there is anything they desire to know, let them ask their husbands at home. For it is shameful for a woman to speak in church" (I Corinthians 14:33–35).

Paul gave no explicit prohibition against premarital sex, but there is one passage which seems to indicate that he did oppose it: "If anyone thinks that he is not behaving properly toward his betrothed, if his passions are strong, and it has to be, let him do as he wishes; let them marry—it is no sin" (I Corinthians 7:36).

Paul was strong in his denunciation of prostitution: "Do you know that your bodies are members of Christ? Shall I therefore take the members of Christ and make them members of a prostitute? Never! Do you not know that he who joins himself to a prostitute becomes one body with her?" (I Corinthians 6: 15–16).

Paul did not write systematically about sex, the position of women, and the role of the family. However, by selecting fragments from his letters to various churches in response to particular problems, a synthesis emerges, and that synthesis is overwhelmingly harmful to the role of women and to the positive value of sex. To be sure, Paul had a strong conviction that Christ would return again soon and, therefore, permanent human relations were not necessary and could even be damaging to the eternal relationship that Christians would have with Christ. Nevertheless, it is still apparent that Paul viewed woman as inferior to man, that he preferred the single over the married state because of the shortness of the time remaining, and that sex to him was a necessary evil that could be tolerated only in the marriage relationship and then only under certain conditions. Although his views were in part a response to the permissiveness and immoralities of his time, they also were his deep religious convictions. Sex had to do with the sins of the flesh which he abhorred. Here is an important difference between Jewish and Pauline attitudes. Judaism had no dominant concept of a future life and did not feel it necessary to repress the pleasures of the flesh for the sake of a future life in the spirit. Paul, however, denounced the earthly pleasures as sinful and urged renunciation for the sake of a greater glory. Paul's letters indicate that he had great difficulty convincing many of his gentile converts of his ascetic beliefs (I Thessalonians 4:2–8, I Corinthians 7:29).

Most of the rest of the New Testament reflects Paul's views: "Women should adorn themselves modestly and sensibly in seemly apparel, not with braided hair or gold or pearls or costly attire but by good deeds as befits women who profess religion. Let a woman learn in silence with all submissiveness. I permit no woman to teach or to have authority over men; she is to keep silent. For Adam was formed first, then Eve; and Adam was not deceived, but the woman was deceived and became a transgressor. Yet woman will be saved through bearing children, if she continues in faith and love and holiness, with modesty" (I Timothy 2:9–15).

Those who shall eventually inherit the earth will not have defiled themselves with women, for they will have remained chaste (Revelation 14:4), a judgment which is more ascetic even than Paul's. It was inevitable that a Christian attitude toward sex and marriage would in large part be shaped in contrast to the moral degradation of Greco-Roman society. What was unfortunate was that these attitudes became so rigid and established as to remain normative for the church in the centuries to come. Eschatology turned into asceticism when Christ did not reappear.

THE EARLY CHURCH

Most of the early church fathers were not encouraging about marriage, considering it a necessary evil to contain sexual relations. Fornication outside of marriage, bloodshed, and apostasy were the three worst sins. Women were second-class citizens. Clement of Rome (A.D. c. 96) declared that the role of the woman was housekeeper: ". . . and the women ye charged to perform all their duties in a blameless and seemly and pure conscience, cherishing their own husbands, as is meet; and yet taught them to keep the role of obedience, and to manage the affairs of their household in seemliness, with all discretion." [5]

The *Epistle to Diognetus* (c. 150) indicated that Christian women were held in higher esteem than their non-Christian counterparts. The Christians "marry like all other men and they beget children; but they do not cast away their offspring. They have their meals in common, but not their wives." [6]

Gradually the idea became more deeply imbedded, a view advocated by the Stoic Musonius, that the only real purpose to sex and marriage was the procreation of children. Any other purpose was a capitulation to the sins of the flesh of mortal man. The ascetic strain in Christian practice became more pronounced. The rise of monasticism led to a denial of the flesh in order that the pure life of the spirit could be attained. Yet Christians stood against Gnostics and Manichees who condemned sex completely.

Clement of Alexandria (c. 150) showed a definite preference for celibacy, although he recognized that marriage would be the best alternative for the majority of people. Men and women are equal in spiritual things, but on the more mundane matters the woman's place is in the home to serve her husband: "We do not say that woman's nature is the same as man's, as she is woman. For undoubtedly it stands to reason that some difference should exist between each of them in virtue of which one is male and the other female. . . . As then there is sameness, as far as respects the soul, she will attain to the same virtue; but as there is difference as respects the peculiar construction of the body, she is destined for childbearing and housekeeping." [7]

Clement was convinced that in these teachings he was following the spirit of the New Testament. Origen (b. 185) declared that women are inferior and that virginity and celibacy are definitely higher than marriage: "God has allowed us to marry, because all are not fit for the higher, that is, the perfectly pure life." [8] Marriage was for the weak in spirit.

One of the most outspoken of all the early Christian thinkers on these matters was Tertullian (b. 160). He firmly believed that the end of the world was near and that this demanded a high standard of conduct for all Christians. He linked the inferiority of woman to the Fall: "Do you not know that you are each an Eve? The sentence of God on this sex of yours lives in this age; the guilt must of necessity live too. *You* are the devil's gateway; *you* are the unsealer of that tree; *you* are the first deserter of the divine law; *you* are she who persuaded him whom the devil was not valiant enough to attack. *You* destroyed so easily God's image, man. On account of *your* desert—that is, death—even the Son of God had to die." [9]

Thus, woman was the reason for man's sin and his fall. Although the sins of the pagans are far worse—sexual immorality, incest, and the like—Christian woman still is as guilty as all other women in causing the Fall. And if first marriages were considered bad, second marriages were little better than bigamy. Tertullian referred to such marriages as "obstructive to holiness" and "detrimental to faith." Yet despite this condemnation of woman, Tertullian could describe eloquently the joys of a good marriage: "Where the flesh is one, one also is the spirit. Together husband and wife pray, together perform their fasts, mutually teaching, exhorting, sustaining. Equally they are found in the church of God, equally at the banquet of God, equally in persecutions and in refreshments. Neither conceals from the other, shuns the other, or is burdensome to the other. Between the two echo psalms and hymns while they mutually challenge each other which shall better sing to their Lord." [10]

But such eloquence should not detract from Tertullian's insistence that woman is inferior: "It is not permitted to a woman to speak in the church; but neither is it permitted her to teach, nor to baptize, nor to offer, nor to claim to herself a lot in any manly function, not to say sacerdotal office." [11]

The early church insisted that the role of the wife should be confined to the home. Girls were reared in strict privacy, with little education and with the fate of early marriage facing them. Bishop Aylmer (b. 1521) declared that women are of two sorts: "Some of them are wiser, better-learned, discreeter and more constant than a number of men, but another and a worse sort of them are fond, foolish, wanton, flibbergibs, tattlers, triflers, wavering, witless, without council, feeble, careless, rash, proud, dainty, tale-bearers, eavesdroppers, rumour-raisers, evil-tongued, worse-minded, and in every way doltified with the dregs of the devil's dunghill." [12]

The Clementine Homilies of the third century relate, "The chaste woman loves her husband from the heart, embraces, soothes, and pleases him, acts the slave to him, and is obedient to him in all things except when she would be disobedient to God." [13]

Ambrose (b. 340) followed Tertullian in pointing out that "Adam was led to sin by Eve, and not Eve by Adam." And Chrysostom (b. 347), who became a bishop, declared that: "Among all savage beasts none is found so harmful as woman." When a friend of Chrysostom's planned to fall from celibacy and marry a beautiful damsel, Chrysostom wrote him an impassioned letter, which changed the friend's mind. This letter said in part: "The groundwork of this corporeal beauty is nothing else but phlegm and blood and humor and bile, and the fluid of masticated food. . . . If you consider what is stored up inside those beautiful eyes, and that straight nose, and the mouth and cheeks, you will affirm the well-shaped body to be nothing else than a whited sepulchre. . . . More- over, when you see a rag with any of these things on it, such as phlegm, or spittle, you cannot bear to touch it even with the tips of your fingers, nay you cannot endure looking at it; are you then in a flutter of excitement about the storehouses and repositories of these things?" [14]

Both Jerome (b. 347) and Augustine (b. 354) advocated the superior state of celibacy and put marriage at the bottom of the scale of virtue. Marriage served as a refuge for men and women of little faith who lacked the spiritual strength to accept the ascetic life. Jerome's antagonism to marriage made him declare the Apostle John superior to Peter since Peter had married while John remained celibate. According to this standard, then, Peter ended up in last place among the twelve apostles. Jerome tolerated marriage because it provided the world with more potential virgins. Jerome made it clear that love was not one of the highest values in a marriage: "It is disgraceful to love another man's wife at all, or one's own too much. A wise man ought to love his wife with judgment, not with passion. Let a man govern his voluptuous impulses, and not rush headlong into intercourse. . . . He who too ardently loves his wife is an adulterer." [15]

Augustine could see no role for woman if childbearing were eliminated. In his earlier life he had committed the sins of the flesh and knew the power of passion. He once exclaimed: "Give me chastity but not yet!" When he became a Christian, he renounced the sins of the flesh and identified Christian behavior with asceticism. Sex is bad because it involves passion and male aggressiveness; therefore, marriage is good only for procreation and without procreation, it is worthy only as a form of holy companionship. He wrote: "Marriage and fornication are not two evils, the second of which is worse, but marriage and continence are two goods, the second of which is better." [16]

Augustine believed that before the Fall, children could have been conceived without lust, and he went to great lengths to justify how this would have been possible: "In Paradise, then, generative seed would have been sown by the husband

and the wife would have conceived . . . by deliberate choice and not by uncontrollable lust. . . . Human organs, without the excitement of lust, could have obeyed (the) human will for the purposes of parenthood. . . . At a time when there was no unruly lust to excite the organs of generation and when all that was needed was done by deliberate choice, the seminal flow could have reached the womb with as little rupture of the hymen and by the same vaginal ducts as is present the case, in reverse, with the menstrual flux. . . . Perhaps these matters are somewhat too delicate for further discussion." [17]

As time progressed, virginity and celibacy continued to be preferred over marriage. To be sure, marriage eventually became a sacrament of the Roman Church, but it still was an inferior state to celibacy. This is seen clearly in the gradual insistence that the clergy remain celibate. The first thirty-seven popes were under no obligation to celibacy, though most of them voluntarily chose it. Those priests today who argue for the right to marry are on fairly sound historical ground. At a church council in 402, Pope Innocent I decreed that bishops, priests, and deacons should remain unmarried, and later Pope Gregory VI (d. 1048) officially imposed celibacy on the priesthood, a teaching that remains to this day. This was a prohibition only in the Western Church, however, and not in the Eastern Church, which permits marriage of the clergy prior to ordination. By and large, however, celibacy was not enforced, and legal clerical marriages and illicit relationships continued occasionally into the sixteenth century. A candidate for holy orders, if he requested, was permitted to marry with the usual religious and legal ceremonies, and to continue in that state after receiving holy orders. In fact, those who remained single were considered with suspicion.

Because of man's natural sexual impulses, priestly celibacy has often led to homosexuality or to promiscuity. H. C. Lea, in his *History of Sacerdotal Celibacy,* relates that in Germany the number of offspring begat by priests often outnumbered those born in wedlock. Henry III, Bishop of Liège, was known to have begat at least sixty-five children. In some countries, notably Spain and Switzerland, some parishes had to insist that each priest have a concubine to protect wives against priestly visitations. In the twelfth century Pope Honorius II sent Cardinal John Crema to England to stamp out priestly sexual immorality. The Cardinal caused the adoption of a canon affirming clerical celibacy. His influence was short-lived, however, when on that very night he was caught in the company of a courtesan! [18] At the Fourth Lateran Council in 1215, Pope Innocent reaffirmed clerical celibacy, and although there continued to be instances of clerical marriages, the pattern of clerical celibacy remained normative in the Roman Church from that time on.

In the beginning the church accepted the Roman marriage ceremony and customs and only gradually developed her own rites. In the second century the church requested that the Roman rite of marriage be later blessed by a priest. As Ignatius put it: "It becomes both men and women to form their union with the approval of the bishop that their marriage be according to the Lord and not after their own lust." [19]

In 392 Emperor Theodosius forbade all pagan marriage rites. The early church also made prohibitions against certain marriages: Christians were not to marry Jews, the unbaptized or heretics. Copulation with a Jew was considered an act of bestiality, and the Theodosian code in the fourth century branded marriage with a Jew as a capital crime. Infanticide and abortions were considered serious evils. Tertullian even went so far as to try to figure out when the fetus became animate; he decided that it was forty days in the case of the male and eighty days for the female, once again an indication of male superiority. Actually Christianity had little influence on Roman law until it became the state religion in the fourth century. Then Christian influence became largely responsible for tighter restrictions on divorce, for the repeal of laws that penalized celibacy, and for passing laws that deprived the father of many of the powers that he enjoyed over his children and wife. Yet for two hundred years after the time of Constantine, Christian emperors did not even attempt to change the custom allowing divorce by common consent; the tradition was too deeply entrenched. The Emperor Justinian declared that those parties who by common consent agreed to a divorce should enter a monastery, but this was such an unpopular law that it was repealed by his nephew Justinian the Second. Although the Christian prohibitions against divorce were not originally absolute—barrenness and religious incompatibility were sufficient cause—they gradually came to be. As marriage came to assume the importance of a sacrament, divorce was completely prohibited, a view which has been consistently maintained by the Catholic Church to this day. By the Middle Ages only annulment and separation were possible, and this meant proving that the original marriage was invalid.

Whereas the Romans had regarded the betrothal as an agreement which could be broken, by the time of Constantine it had been given legal sanction. The Council of Constantinople in Trullo (680–681) declared that marriage to a betrothed woman while her first betrothed was still alive was tantamount to adultery. However, the betrothal ceremony remained a private affair, with the parents signing an agreement concerning the future bride's dowry. By the ninth century the practice had developed whereby the girl received a betrothal ring for her third finger on her left hand, a result of a romantic notion that a tiny vein linked the heart with this finger. The earliest Christian marriage ritual that is extant dates to about the seventh century. An illustration of a marriage benediction follows: "May she be a faithful and chaste wife in Christ and may she continue a follower of holy women. . . . May she be modest, grave, bashful. . . . May she be fruitful in childbearing." [20] This passage suggests the inferiority and submissiveness of the wife to the husband, her weakness of nature, and her role as child-begetter.

At about the same time, church manuals began to appear which explored the subject of the sex act in great detail, listing every conceivable misdeed with the corresponding penalty. The two general rules were: 1. Celibacy is preferable for laymen, compulsory for priests; 2. Intercourse is prohibited outside of marriage, and inside marriage only for the purpose of procreation. Sometimes fornication was declared worse than murder, but in some manuals the worst sin of all was masturbation. Sexual relationships were for a time illegal on Sundays, Wednesdays, and Fridays. Later the church made sex illicit during Lent, during the three days preceding communion, and during penance. The sex act was to be performed in only one position, with the priest assigning penalties for other variants. A rule of the seventh century insisted that: "Those who are joined together in matrimony should abstain from cohabitation three nights before receiving communion." [21] Sexual intercourse was considered unclean; therefore, married couples must abstain from intercourse for three nights after their marriage, the so-called Tobias nights. Once having performed the sexual act, they were not to enter a church for thirty days, and then only if they agreed to do forty days of penance and bring an offering.

THE MIDDLE AGES AND THE REFORMATION

By the Middle Ages the church had established authority over both marriage and family matters. The norm upheld by the church continued to be that sex was to be avoided at all costs except for purposes of procreation. Aquinas (b. 1224) taught that marriage is good, but that sex in marriage is only for procreation: "Every emission of the semen is contrary to the good of man, which takes place in a way whereby generation is impossible; and if this is done on purpose, it must be a sin." [22] In fact, next to murder, the worst sin was the inordinate emission of semen which precluded conception.

Since sexual liberties were taken by church members, the church often had to compromise her convictions for the sake of keeping some people under her wing. Prostitution was widespread and frequently condoned by the church, Aquinas stating that it was a necessary dimension of social morality in the same way that a cesspool is necessary to a palace, if the whole palace is not to reek. Queen Joanna of Avignon established a brothel, and when King Sigismond visited Constance, he and his court were not at all reluctant to visit the town prostitutes. When Pope Innocent IV left the city of Lyons after a visit of eight years' duration, he said to the citizens: "Since we came here we have effected great improvements. When we came, we found but three or four brothels. We leave behind but one. We must add, however, that it extends without interruption from the eastern to the western gate." [23]

Many of the popes of this period were known for their sexual exploits. John XII turned St. John Lateran into a brothel, and his successor Leo VIII is reported to have been fatally stricken in the act of adultery. Balthasar Cossa, who was elected pope to end the Great Schism, while still a cardinal lived in Bologna, "where two hundred maids, matrons and widows, including a few nuns, fell victims to his brutal lust." [24]

The official view of the church, however, was far different. A man should not even love his wife since this might lead to lust; however, there were movements in the church that opposed this unromantic view. In southern France in the twelfth century, new developments in male-female relationships occurred, one of which was the courts of love. Women became idealized, and love became worthy. To be sure, courtly love was not supposed to be achieved in marriage, which meant that adultery became necessary for the fulfillment of romance.

Nevertheless, this notion of romantic love was a new dimension quite apart from usual church practice. Courtly love had its own built-in tyrannies against woman. It put her on a pedestal, celebrated her differences, and made her an object of male passion. This image of woman as a love object was just as damning as her inferior role in the church.

The Renaissance, with its stress on the individual, did represent some improvement for the lot of woman although this was restricted largely to the higher social classes. These women were given more opportunities in education and in social relationships. But the typical attitude remained that woman was inferior to man, a view illustrated by Castiglioni, who in 1528 extolled the abilities of woman by saying: "all things that men can understand, the same can women understand too." Therefore, a lady's knowledge should include "letters, music, painting, and how to dance and make merry." [25] A classical education was still denied women since they were deemed incapable of it. Moreover, the Renaissance did not help women on the more important matters of legal and economic rights. Legally the rule remained: "Husband and wife are one, and the husband is the one."

Very little progress in attitudes toward sex and marriage was made during the period of the early Reformation as the Reformers were more interested in other issues. Previously the Lollards, followers of John Wyclif in England in the fourteenth century, had petitioned Parliament to denounce clerical celibacy. On the other hand, another leading pre-Reformer, John Hus of Bohemia, insisted on clerical celibacy. Martin Luther (b. 1485), the major figure in the early Reformation of the sixteenth century, did present some novel ideas on marriage that helped to break some of the former restrictions. Most important was the notion that marriage could be superior to celibacy.

Luther wrote: "There are three kinds of love, false, natural and married. False love is that which seeks its own, just as one loves gold, goods, honor, or women outside of matrimony contrary to God's command. Natural love is between father and children, brother and sister, et cetera. But above them all is married love, that is, a bride's love. It burns as fire, and seeks nothing more than the mate. It says, 'I wish not yours, I wish neither gold nor silver, neither this nor that. I want only you, I want everything or nothing.' All other loves seek something else than that which is love, but this love alone desires the beloved completely. If Adam had not fallen, the love of the bridegroom and the bride would be the loveliest thing. But now love is not pure, because although the married partner seeks the other yet the desire of self enters in and perverts this love." [26]

Luther believed that marriage should be essentially a civil matter, declaring in his *Table Talk* that marriage, being "a temporal and worldly thing, does not concern the church." [27] A sacrament must be instituted by Christ; marriage was not. Therefore, marriage was more a matter for the state than the church. As a result the provinces in Germany gradually assumed responsibility for marriage although the practice of having a public ceremony in the church remained. Marriage became a civil contract, solemnized by either church or state; however, in England, church marriage continued to be the practice. Luther further affirmed that betrothals were to be considered obligatory if they were publicly made with parental consent although they should not be consummated until after the marriage had been solemnized. Luther opposed divorce, stating he would even prefer bigamy. However, he recognized the power of the civil court to grant divorce for reasons of adultery, desertion, and the like.

Luther abolished clerical celibacy, largely because of the prevailing clerical promiscuity. Luther's rationale was that the clergy should marry because they required housekeepers, and to put a single priest in the same house with a woman would be like putting straw next to fire and not expecting it to burn. Luther encouraged nuns to leave the cloister, he himself marrying one, Katherine von Bora. Luther's attitude toward his own wife was contradictory. At one time he said of her: "My wife is more precious to me than the Kingdom of France and all the treasures of Venice." [28] Yet a year later he exclaimed: "Get you a wife and then your mind, however fuzzy it is, will become straight as a ribbon; it will be reduced to one idea: Do and think as *she* wishes." [29] One time he could exult: "I love my Kate, and know that I love her more than she loves me." [30] And yet in the next breath he would moan: "If I were to marry again I would carve myself an obedient wife out of stone, for to find one of flesh and blood is not conceivable." [31]

He apparently found the sexual side of marriage satisfying, for he declared that sex was as natural as eating. Sex in itself is not sinful; sin consists in the selfish use of sex. Yet he had ambivalent feelings, saying: "Had God consulted me about it, I should have advised Him to continue the generation of the species by fashioning human beings out of clay, as Adam was made." [32] The role of the wife was to bear children and take care of the home: "Take women from their housewifery and they are good for nothing." [33]

Luther's views toward sex and marriage eventually became widely accepted. For him the father was the absolute head of the house: ". . . the woman's will, as God says, shall be subject to the man, and he shall be her master." [34] The father was the master, and the children were to be obedient to him. Luther looked upon the family as a school for character. Women, he said, should stay at home because they have large hips and should sit on them. Marriages should be arranged by the parents. Luther recognized that no marriage is always smooth. He once exclaimed: "Good God, what a lot of trouble there is in marriage! Adam has made a mess of our nature. Think of all the squabbles Adam and Eve must have had in the course of their nine hundred years. Eve would say,

'You ate the apple,' and Adam would retort, 'You gave it to me.' " [35]

Luther and his wife had six children, and they were expected to be obedient to their father at all times. He loved his children yet his volatile temperament made him oscillate between severity and compassion. One time he complained: "Christ said we must become as little children to enter the kingdom of heaven. Dear God, this is too much. Have we got to become such idiots?" [36]

Calvin's (b. 1509) views were similar to Luther's. The purpose of marriage was for procreation and to restrain the sexual appetite. Sex within marriage was permissible if carefully controlled. Adultery was punishable by death or banishment. Calvin once suggested that God had ordained syphilis to punish the promiscuous. Calvin himself married the widow of an Anabaptist in 1559. Erasmus, the great humanist of the early Reformation period, came out in favor of clerical marriages as a means of lessening sexual immorality on the part of the clergy, many of whom kept concubines or practiced homosexuality. Ulrich Zwingli, the founder of the Reformed Protestant movement in Switzerland, argued that since God had ordained marriage, it is proper for everyone including priests. Zwingli himself married a widow in 1524. The Church of England came out in favor of clerical marriage in 1549, an act that was repealed by Queen Mary in 1553 but reluctantly reintroduced by Queen Elizabeth in 1559.

The left-wing Reformers de-emphasized the value of sex, even in marriage. For example, Thomas Muentzer taught abstinence in marriage except for procreation. The Anabaptists tended to treat marriage as a spiritual union which lasted for eternity and to disparage the union of the flesh. They were unalterably opposed to divorce and remarriage. They further believed that a marriage between an Anabaptist and a non-Anabaptist was no marriage at all, and that if the unbelieving spouse could not be converted, then the marriage could be ended. Some of the Anabaptists practiced polygyny, others rejected private property and had wives in common.

Celibacy for the clergy in the Catholic Church was re-affirmed at the Council of Trent in the sixteenth century. Prior to the Council of Trent the Catholic Church had admitted that in the early church clerical celibacy was not widely observed; now, however, they took great pains to prove that celibacy was dictated by both scripture and tradition. The Council declared anathema anyone who said that priests, monks, and nuns could marry and further anathematized those who believed that marriage was superior to virginity.

LATER DEVELOPMENTS

Women's legal status remained virtually the same from the fifteenth to the nineteenth century. Any improvement was confined to the privileged classes where women were given more freedom. Even Rousseau in the eighteenth century could say that: "Women's entire education should be relative to men—woman was made to yield to man and to put up with his injustice." [37] The churches, both Catholic and Protestant, continued to perpetuate the idea that women were inferior, that their role was confined to the home, that sex was primarily for procreation. The church hierarchy, priests and ministers, all were men. The policy of the churches continued to be one of sexual repression, and they sought to impose these standards on others. Pope Leo XIII, in his encyclical on Christian marriage in 1880, reaffirmed the inferiority of the wife: "The husband is the chief of the family and the head of the wife. The woman, because she is flesh of his flesh and bone of his bone, must be subject to her husband and obey him; not, indeed, as a servant, but as a companion, so that her obedience shall be wanting in neither honor nor dignity." [38] This was the dominant view of the Christian churches throughout the nineteenth century. The changes in the attitude toward marriage, family, and sex which slowly began to take place in the present century were made in spite of and not because of the church.

Woman continued to be treated as an inferior being and the patriarchal pattern of family life remained firmly established. The father-husband was the oracle of authority and considered himself the sole breadwinner, with his children and wife subservient to him. During the eighteenth and nineteenth centuries there existed a household economy, with the Europeans using the same type of plough and loom that had been used for over two thousand years. Handwork was the basis of industry, and wife and children were apprentices to the head of the house. The normal household routine of the mother, in addition to caring for children and husband, might have included weaving and spinning yarn, curing meat and baking bread, preserving fruit and brewing beer. However, a greater supply of goods for an expanding trade became necessary and consequently new methods had to be devised for increasing production. The proliferation of factories with their manufactured goods meant not only the end of the domestic system of producing goods, but also the urbanization of the population. Workers clustered near their place of work, the factory. Between the end of the seventeenth century and the 1920s, the percentage of people in England living in cities increased from 20 percent to 80 percent. This urbanization of the population was true all over Europe.

Since women and children were considered inferior to men, they could be employed for lower wages. Each job in the factory was a special type of work which could easily be performed by almost anyone regardless of age or sex. Men lost their jobs, and this trend contributed to the breakdown of family life. Women who worked for sixteen hours a day in a factory had neither time nor energy for domestic life. Children who worked similar long hours had no close parental ties to nurture and guide them. Homes became abodes for sleep, with little time for genuine communication among members. The family became less and less important to the individual as far as his welfare was concerned. Eventually the state stepped in to ameliorate the working conditions and hours. An act of 1802 in England limited the number of hours that children could work to twelve a day and compelled their employers to provide better working conditions and improved sleeping quarters. As working hours for children were shortened, compulsory schooling increased, keeping the children away from the home. Indeed, the emphasis on education for children actually established a new adolescent stage in life, with the emphasis on training for adulthood. Whereas the child previous to this time was considered grown up at a very early age and took his place in society, he now was withdrawn from adult society for a period to receive special training. By 1850 in England women were not permitted to work in a factory except between the hours of 6:00 A.M. and 6:00 P.M., precisely the hours when small children most needed their mothers at home.

The Industrial Revolution thus contributed to the breakdown of family stability. On the positive side it helped to free both women and children from economic dependence on the husband or father.

Punitive laws that prohibited women from owning property and from appearing as equals with men in the courts of law were removed. In 1870 the Married Women's Property Act gave married women control over their own earnings, and in 1882 Parliament enacted a law giving women entire control over their property. Women found increasing leisure time, even time to be educated! The mother's rights to her own children came more slowly. Until 1886 English law declared that the father had exclusive authority over his children, and indeed it was not until 1925 that a law was enacted which gave equal rights to both mother and father concerning the guardianship of infants.

The role of the church as an instrument of social control in

Europe and the United States began to lessen as religious skepticism spread. Many church people no longer accepted with certainty the supernatural claims of the church as society questioned old dogmas and doubted the standards of conduct imposed by religious authorities. The church refused to bend with the times. Andrew White's *A History of the Warfare Between Science and Theology* is a precise documentation of the fierce resistance of the church to human progress in most spheres of life. The inevitable result was the diminishing role that the church played in the life of society. Only in very recent years have some churches begun to rethink their stand on matters relating to sex, marriage, and the family. This process of secularization was part of the movement toward the breakdown of external authority and the rapidly growing trend toward individualization. The old agents of social control—the clan, the family, the church, the school—lost their influence.

What we see, then, in the nineteenth century is the beginning of the transformation of the role of the woman and the character of family life. The wife began to achieve certain rights of her own as a human being. The patriarchal notion of the family, which had persisted since ancient times, began to weaken; new patterns of family living appeared. In short, what has happened is that man has sharply decreased his dependence on the traditional family structure for the fulfillment of his wants and desires. Economic, social, educational, and recreational needs are no longer exclusive functions of the family.

This change in the pattern of family living has led to a serious challenge to monogamous marriage, the nuclear family, and the procreative function of sex. Although the patriarchal form of the family still persists in many Western countries, and although woman still has not achieved equal dignity with man, the trend is unmistakable. New forms of marriage, family living, and sexual relationships are emerging. There is passing the "great family," which maintained a closely knit group of relatives with the reverence of common traditions. The desire for marriage is now expressed in terms of love and romance rather than economic security. And the norm of sexual behavior is shaped more by pleasure than by procreation. But before we examine these new attitudes, we need to look more closely at what has happened in the United States.

Two

THE
AMERICAN WAY

Edward N. Saveth has recently pointed out that very little research has been conducted on the history of the American family. Although many theories have been presented as to the nature and development of the family, the evidence is minimal. As Saveth suggests: "Actually, there are so many families that one can prove almost anything about family experience in general." [1] John Demos's study *A Little Commonwealth: Family Life in Plymouth Colony* stresses the paucity of information and the lack of uniformity in family living. [2] All that we can do, then, is to suggest trends that seem to be consistent with the little knowledge we do have.

New England and the Puritan Influence

The pattern of family living and sexual mores in the early American colonies had its source in the traditions and customs of the English Puritans and other groups that emigrated from Europe. These colonists, in seeking to build a holy commonwealth in the new world, brought with them particular ideas about the role of the family, the mother, and the child. The cardinal affirmation of Puritanism was the religious basis of all phases of life. No facet of a person's or a community's life could escape the influence of God's holy will.

The Puritans believed that God had made a special covenant with his people which involved definite and specific obligations and standards of conduct derived from the Bible. The church was at the center of the religious, intellectual, social, and recreational life of the colony, even though not all inhabitants were church members. Daily Bible reading and family prayers were regular activities. God's mandate included the entire household, as Thomas Shepard indicated in pointing out the need for Sabbath observance: ". . . our children, servants, strangers who are within our gates, are apt to profane the Sabbath; we are therefore to improve our power over them for God, in restraining them from sin, and in constraining them (as far as we can) to the holy observance of the rest of the sabbath, lest God impute their sins to us. . . ." [3]

The Puritans believed that God had carefully arranged human society into an hierarchical order of human relationships. Old were superior to young, parents to children, men to women, rich to poor, educated to uneducated, and craftsmen to daily laborers. As God rules over men, so do men rule over women and parents over children. As men were submissive to their divine Master, so should wives be obedient to their husbands. Civil government exercised control, and church and state worked hand in hand.

Families constituted the center of God's divine hierarchy of human relationships. In practice this meant a division of responsibilities in the difficult work of settling in the wilderness and later on the frontier. Men toiled in field and forest, women managed the household, and children helped where they were so ordered; the family shared the hardships and loneliness of the settlements. Although women lacked the status of men, they did not necessarily find this inhibiting or humiliating. They had too many other interests which were time-consuming, and indeed in some areas such as the teaching of religion and education, literature and art, they often played the dominant role. Until the twentieth century the mother was a necessary productive agent with the father in making a living and doing the necessary chores. As long as she had this productive function, her sphere was unquestionably in the home.

The father reigned as head of the house and absolute in authority, in theory if not always in practice. The mother occupied herself with household chores, bore a large number of children, and served her husband. This living pattern was usually the best that she could hope for. Although in 1790 the average number of children per family in the American colonies was 5.8, families of ten to twelve children were not unusual. A poet friend of Mrs. Sara Thayer, who died in 1751, wrote:

> Also, she was a fruitful vine,
> the truth I may relate—
> Fourteen was of her body born
> And lived to man's estate.

> From these did spring a numerous race,
> One hundred thirty-two;
> Sixty and six each sex alike,
> As I declare to you.

> And one thing more remarkable,
> Which I shall here record:
> She'd fourteen children with her
> At the table of our Lord.[4]

When a woman married, she surrendered her property and any money she earned to her husband. She had little standing in the courts of law, could not serve on juries nor vote; she was not even considered educable. Indeed, it was commonly believed that woman's brain was smaller than man's. When the wife of Governor Hopkins went insane in the eighteenth century, Governor Winthrop attributed her condition to the fact that she read and wrote too much: "Her husband, being very loving and tender of her, was loath to grieve her; but he saw his error, when it was too late. For, if she had attended her household affairs, and such things as belong to women, and not gone out of her way and calling to meddle in such things as are proper to men, whose minds are stronger, etc., she had kept her wits, and might have improved them usefully and honorably in the place God had set her." [5] Clergymen supported this view with quotations from the Bible and prayers uttered to God. However, a husband was by law responsible for his wife's support and was not permitted to strike her, abuse her, or use "hard words" against her under penalty of the law.

MARRIAGE A CIVIL CONTRACT

In New England, marriage was a civil contract, as it had become in England during Cromwell's reign. Although the Hardwicke Act of 1753 again made marriage in England a religious ceremony with but a few exceptions, the pattern in New England remained basically a civil one; thus, marriage and the family continued to be religious in spirit and tradition, but secular by law. The promises were made orally as they are today, and in some cases, self-betrothals were made without any later formal marriage ceremony. Some couples were fined monthly until they had a legal marriage ceremony. The Massachusetts Bay Colony insisted that the wedding ceremony be performed by a civil magistrate, and at first clergymen were not permitted to deliver a sermon at the wedding, a custom that continued until 1686. This anticlerical attitude died out when the danger of ecclesiastical control from England had been eliminated. The colony of Rhode Island, founded for religious freedom, was so suspicious of clerical intervention that it did not permit clergymen of all denominations to officiate at marriages until 1733. Probably because marriage was a civil affair, the New England colonies were willing to grant divorces for such reasons as desertion, impotence, adultery, and cruelty. The Puritans considered marriage to be a blessing from God. This was true no matter how bad the particular marriage happened to be. As John Cotton put it: "Women are Creatures without which there is no comfortable living for man; it is true of them what is wont to be said of Governments, That bad ones are better than none; They are a sort of Blasphemers then who despise and decry them, and call them a necessary Evil, for they are a necessary Good; such as it was not good that man should be without." [6]

The love of God was the first prerequisite to a successful marriage. Love between man and woman was secondary and more dutiful than romantic, and the decision to marry was often made without any prospective partner in sight. In that case social rank and availability were prime factors, far more important than love and romance. Sometimes a man would advertise for a wife. In the *Boston Evening Post* of February, 1759, appeared this plea: "To the ladies. Any young lady between the ages of 18 and 23 of a midling stature; brown hair, regular features and a lively brisk eye: of good morals and not tinctured with anything that may sully so distinguished a form, possessed of 300 or 400 pounds entirely at her disposal and where there will be no necessity of going through the tiresome talk of addressing parents or guardians for their consent: such a one by leaving a line directed for A. W. at the British Coffee House in King Street appointing where an interview may be had will meet with a person who flatters himself he shall not be thought disagreeable by any lady answering the above description. N. B. Profound secrecy will be observed. No trifling answers will be regarded." [7] Puritan love ended at the death of one of the marriage partners. Remarriage was usually accomplished swiftly, and widows were fair game inasmuch as they had usually inherited one-third of their deceased husband's property and because they were in great abundance.

Celibacy was frowned upon, and bachelors in particular were discriminated against; indeed, they were virtually suspect as criminals. If a bachelor could not set up a household of his own, he was expected to live with another family and be subject to its customs and discipline. If he refused to find such a family, the civil authorities found one for him. In 1636 Connecticut declared that ". . . noe young man that is neither mated nor hath any servaunte, and be noe publicke officer, shall keep howse by himself, without consent of the Towne where he lives first had, under paine of 20s. per weeke." [8]

Unmarried women usually lived with their parents or a married brother or sister, assisting them in the raising of the large family. Poems such as "The Bachelors' Last Shift" and an "Epigram on An Old Maid Who Married Her Servant" poked fun at the single person. The woman's role, married or not, was in the home, and for nearly 150 years after the first landing of the pilgrims, women wage earners were virtually confined to domestic work.

The Puritans shared the dominant Christian attitude that sex is essentially for procreation. Marriage served the purpose of controlling the sexual urge within definite limitations. This emphasis on the limitations of sex led to the identification of sin and sex as one and the same. Puritan moral standards have remained dominant in this country from earliest days. Although these standards were often broken, their validity was not seriously questioned until this century. This meant that chastity before marriage and fidelity during marriage were practiced by the majority. The suppression of sex as a pleasurable activity and as a natural outlet for aggression has been suggested as the chief explanation for the cause of outbreaks of witchcraft hysteria and similar phenomena in colonial times. Women were blamed for most of the manifestations of evil spirits in which people of that period so devoutly believed. Massachusetts law stated that women who were suspected of practicing witchcraft should be stripped and their bodies examined by a male "witch-pricker" for evidence of the mark of the devil.

But Puritans were only human, and since to err is human, their actions did not always match their words. In 1670 John Smith was fined ten pounds and ordered by the court to return to his wife after he had taken off with another woman. The court admonished Elizabeth Wheeler and Joanna Pierce for sitting in the laps of men other than their husbands. The church censured Abigail Bush for referring to her father's second wife as "hot as a bitch." Jacob Minline and Sarah Tuttle were hauled before the court because in the presence of others they had ". . . sat down together, his arm being about her, and her arm upon his shoulder or about his neck; and he kissed her and she kissed him, or they kissed one another, continuing in this posture about half an hour." [9] Jacob was found innocent, but Sarah was fined for being a "bold virgin," an indication of the double standard. Adultery was considered a serious offense and a prime cause for divorce. Punishment for adulterers ranged from fines and whippings to wearing the letter "A." However, the Puritans did not believe that adultery made men and women equally guilty in the eyes of the law; the man was still favored. In one case in 1707 in Plymouth, the guilty woman received thirty lashes and was forced to wear the letter "A" for the rest of her life while the man was acquitted.

Custom favored late marriage and a short engagement.

Girls married usually at about twenty years of age and boys around twenty-five. The age for marriage began to drop after the colonial period. Child marriages, so common in England at the time, were not the practice in the colonies. Before a couple could be married, an announcement of the impending marriage had to be made at three public meetings in succession or by written notice posted in a public place. In several of the New England colonies an engaged couple was considered as good as married even though the actual marriage had not finally been legalized. The betrothal period served as a trial period for the couple to get to know each other better. Engaged couples who had sexual relations and were discovered were not punished as severely as others as long as they were eventually married, unless a child was conceived before marriage. The Plymouth statutes of 1671 declared that ordinary fornicators should be fined ten pounds while engaged couples were fined only half that amount. Until 1803, in some areas of New England, a couple who had a child born less than seven months after marriage had to confess their indiscretion before their church congregation. Cases of premarital sex were numerous. The records of the Groton, Connecticut, church note that of two hundred baptized members between 1761 and 1775, sixty-six confessed to fornication before marriage. Fornication seemed to be the most popular sin in Puritan New England, which indicates that times have not changed. Governor Bradford in 1642 complained of conditions at Plymouth: ". . . not only incontinence between persons unmarried, for which many both men and women have been punished sharply enough but some married persons also." [10] If the engagement was broken, the offended one could sue for breach of promise. Parents normally approved the marriage of their children although the young people were given some freedom of choice. As late as 1756, Connecticut gave to parents the legal right to arrange marriages for their children.

Many marriages were arranged with the economic factor

as a primary consideration. When Luce Downing was persuaded by her money-minded parents to marry a certain wealthy Mr. Norton, her father wrote delightedly: "She may stay long ere she meet with a better unless I had more money for her than I now can spare." [11] Benjamin Franklin in 1721 lampooned economic marriage as follows:

A Swarm of Sparks, young, gay, and bold,
Lov'd Sylvia long, but she was cold;
Int'rest and pride the nymph control'd,
So they in vain their passion told.
At last came Dulman, he was old,
Nay, he was ugly, but had gold,
He came, and saw, and took the hold,
While t'other beaux their loss consol'd.
Some say, she's wed; I say she's sold. [12]

Franklin, in his *Reflections on Courtship and Marriage,* included Jonathan Swift's "Letter to a Very Young Lady on Her Marriage," which recommended that she be modest and reserved in her marriage, undemonstrative toward her husband in public and never hysterically possessive.

Bundling was an ancient practice that found new favor in colonial times. Originally it was confined to the lower economic classes. Houses were small, beds were scarce and wayfarers had to be accommodated. The Abbé Robin, who visited Connecticut in 1788, reported: "The Americans of these parts are very hospitable; they have commonly but one bed in the house, and the chaste spouse, although she were alone, would divide it with her guest, without hesitation or fear." [13] Bundling as an acceptable practice began to disappear as houses became bigger and beds more abundant. However, young people were quick to see the amorous advantages to this practice. At Harvard College in the early days one of the favorite topics for debate was "whether it be Fornication to Lye with ones Sweetheart (after contraction) before Marriage." The church attempted to prevent this practice, but her pleas were often thwarted, and, moreover, public confession of amorous bundling often brought forth more merriment than punishment.

Children, legally speaking, were chattel of their parents. The children were reared under strict discipline, a result in large part of Calvinist teachings about the depravity of man. They were expected to obey their parents above all else. As the Pilgrim preacher John Robinson put it: "There is in all children a stubbornness and stoutness of mind arising from natural pride which must in the first place be broken and beaten down." [14] The courts enforced strict discipline. The prevailing social code obligated parents to provide adequately for their children. Childhood was short; a boy usually chose his calling between age ten and fourteen, and at the age of sixteen, he began paying taxes. For the next several years he served as an apprentice before launching out on his own. In many cases, parents sent their children out at an early age to live in other homes, possibly to prevent the parents from showing undue affection. This was also a way of separating the child from home at the time he began to assert his independence. Education was voluntary and centered in the home; not until the eighteenth century did formal schooling become widespread.

Thus, colonial Americans derived their ideas about marriage and family life from English custom, with a few notable exceptions. The law protected the wife from abuse by her husband. Boys and girls had more freedom together before marriage and more independence in determining their marriage partners. Civil divorce was widely practiced. The United States developed a pattern of family living that was more in tune with a new world of independence and religious and social heterogeneity. Even so, the basic patriarchal family pattern upheld for centuries by the church remained the same. This New England family pattern, as one commentator has noted: ". . . had more to do with the shaping of our national culture than did that of any other colonial region or that of any subsequent immigrant group." [15]

The Middle Colonies and the South

A more heterogeneous population characterized the middle colonies, and generalities about attitudes toward sex, marriage, and family life are difficult to make. In the Dutch colony of New Netherlands the practice had continued of long betrothals, which often meant sexual union without marriage. Finally in 1658, a law stipulated that man and woman could not live together as man and wife until they had been legally married. Another law discouraged long betrothal by requiring marriage within a month after the publication of banns. The higher social classes often would disregard the banns and get special permission from the governor to marry. Couples married early and often too hastily, and there was discrimination against bachelors and spinsters. The role of the woman was to fulfill her household duties although there were women in early times who were merchants, shippers, and even Indian traders; frontier experiences encouraged expansion of the female role. Divorce was frowned upon, and in the century preceding the Revolution there was no recorded divorce in the colony of New York. Dutch women often received a better education than their New England counterparts, and family life was somewhat more lax, a reflection perhaps of the more tolerant spirit of Dutch Protestantism as contrasted with Calvinist teachings dominant in New England.

In New Jersey most of the colonists were Presbyterians or Congregationalists and therefore more deeply influenced by New England customs. Women belonged in the home, and the education they received was essentially domestic. In 1719 the New Jersey Legislature prohibited marriage for persons under the age of 21 without the consent of parents or guardians. Adultery was usually punished by whipping or banishment. New Jersey and Delaware contained a great mixture of different settlements living in close proximity. This intermingling and intermarriage led to a liberalization of marriage and divorce practices and was also an unsettling menace to the traditional structure of family life. Pennsylvania exhibited the same breadth and tolerance.

In the South, marriage enjoyed high esteem, was traditional in terms of the role of father, mother, and children and was usually made at an early age. Family life in Virginia was patriarchal in character, with a woman enjoying a larger measure of freedom that was for the most part, however, confined to the home. This freedom was primarily due to the economic situation and the climate, which was easier to adjust to than the more severe weather and environment of New England. Southern chivalry did not date back to the earliest settlements. The southern colonies were more bourgeois than aristocratic. Indeed, for all the minor regional variations, there were no really significant differences among sections of the country in the manner in which women were treated or in the degree to which they took up independent careers. The difference was more in terms of exigencies of the particular situation than in any differing view of the nature of woman.

At the end of the Revolutionary period, James Franklin wrote that for the most part Virginia ladies: ". . . chiefly spend their time in sewing and taking care of their families; for they seldom read or endeavor to improve their minds. However, they are in general good housewives; and tho they have not perhaps so much tenderness and sensibility as the English ladies, yet they make as good wives and as good mothers as any in the world." [16]

Most people married at a younger age than in New England. Chief Justice Marshall fell in love with his wife when she was but fourteen and married her two years later. One report observed: "They marry generally very young, some at 13 or 14, and she that continues unmarried until 20, is reckoned a stale maid, which is a very different character in that country." [17] With girls marrying so young, there was little chance for premarital experience. Most marriages within the aristocratic families were arranged with parental supervision. The Church of England for a long time prescribed the proper marriage ceremony, and in some of the southern colonies ecclesiastical marriage was for many years compulsory. Only gradually did marriage in the South become a civil matter, ironically at about the time that marriage in New England became more of an ecclesiastical matter. In the early days no southern colony had tribunals authorized to permit divorce, and not a case has been found of divorce being permitted by pre-Revolutionary legislatures. The legislatures did permit separations and annulments, however. This narrow attitude toward divorce was in line with the general conservatism of the South.

A problem that made the situation in the South more complex was the existence of large numbers of Negro slaves. This group was the object of severe abuse on the part of certain of the white gentry, with, of course, no opportunity on the part of the Negroes for equal justice before the law. The double standard was very much a part of southern mores, with the women of the middle and upper social classes expected to remain faithful while their men could be philanderers. Thus white men had easy access to white women of the lower social classes as well as to the black female slaves. Slaves had no legal protection against the white man's promiscuity, and on many of the plantations some of the children of the master were born of black women. The church for the most part condoned this practice, even to the point of declaring that if a minister had a child by a woman not his wife, the church would expel him if she were white but would not punish him if she were black.

Western frontier life was as rigorous as in the early colonial settlements in New England. Men and women needed each other to supplement the work that had to be done. Frontier conditions favored early marriage and many children, because they were needed to do the work of the homestead. Therefore, a typical toast on wedding night would be: "Health to the groom, and here's to the bride, thumping luck, and big children." Pioneer women were usually grandmothers at forty, and mothers and daughters often gave birth to children in the same year. Frontier life tended to lose many of the traditions and customs attached to marriage and sex since there was less parental influence and more freedom from European traditions. The family remained the major social structure in a nation which increasingly stressed the importance of independence and individual initiative. Hierarchical religion and politics were twin enemies of the frontier spirit. Frontier religion had a freeing grace in substituting emotionalism and individualism for ancient dogmas and patterns of behavior. Government was reduced to a minimum, and in some areas of the frontier it was necessary to live without benefit of civil or ecclesiastical authority. Settlements received only occasional visits from ministers; therefore, social control over the family and marriage lessened and sexual mores became more varied and permissive. Indeed, the development of flexible laws with respect to marriage and sex was in large part a response to the new conditions imposed by frontier life.

To be sure, church denominations became anxious about this rampant individualism and laxity of standards and sought to impose restrictions that went beyond civil law, particularly in cases of church members marrying persons outside the church. For example, in 1796, the General Conference of the Methodist Church declared: "We do not prohibit our people from marrying persons who are not of our society, provided such persons have the form and are seeking the power of godliness; but if they marry persons who do not come up to this description, we shall be obliged to purge our society of them. . . . We are well assured that few things have been more pernicious to the work of God than the marriage of the children of God with the children of this world. We therefore think ourselves obliged to bear our testimony, both in doctrine and discipline, against so great an evil." [18]

The movement toward independence from hierarchical government and churches also made divorces more easily obtainable. After the Revolutionary War, divorce by private statute continued for more than half a century in most areas, and only as the government later became more centralized did the laws tend to become more uniform and strict. The churches sought to prevent the breakup of marriage so far as possible, and in the nineteenth century the General Assembly of the Presbyterian Church pointed out to the churches ". . . a tendency manifest in some portions of our country to relax the sacredness of the marriage tie." [19]

Some Changes in the Nineteenth Century

In the nineteenth century the status of children began to improve albeit slowly. Child rearing and education had been largely a family affair until the schools and churches developed in sufficient strength and number. This, together with the fact that parents on the frontier usually had little time to act as fathers and mothers, meant freeing children from home ties. Although patriarchalism remained strong, children did come to maturity at an early age and were able to set off on their own. Children were not nearly as free as their twentieth-century counterparts, but they were considerably more independent than their contemporary European counterparts.

One commentator observed in 1857: "American parents, allowing an almost unlimited choice to their children, spare nevertheless no hardship and pains to bring them up, and to educate them according to their conception of what is the best and the most useful for the mature duties of life. Parents love their children as dearly and intensely here as in Europe, but exercise less control, less authority. . . . Even in the serious decisions of life, children in America enjoy a fullness of independence not customary in Europe. They make freely the choice of their intimacies, then of their church, of their politics, their husbands and wives." [20]

This movement toward independence was inevitable in a country whose pluralistic style of living was pragmatic, heterogeneous, and individualistic. Obviously to many people it appeared as though the old foundations of family and marriage were being destroyed. Indeed they were, but in their place there was beginning to develop an attitude toward family and marriage based more on companionship and love than tradition and authority.

In the nineteenth century the education of women began to take on greater importance. Before 1800 most of the education for girls and women was limited to a few months a year and confined to such subjects as music, dancing, and needlework. The real purpose of female education was to gain husbands and learn how to manage children and maintain homes. Rousseau expressed the prevailing attitude toward female education: "The education of women should be always relative to the men. To please, to be useful to us, to make us love and esteem them, to educate us when young and to take care of us when grown old, to advise, to console us, to render our lives easy and agreeable; these are the duties of women at all times." [21]

When a girl was given a public examination in geometry in New York State in 1829, there was a large chorus of disapproval, "the clergy, as usual, prophesying the dissolution of all family bonds." [22] When the suggestion was first made that Elmira College be founded for women, one professor exclaimed: "I am informed that a charter has just been issued in New York State for the forming of a women's college and that a foolish effort is being made to place young women on the platform before an audience. To my mind this borders on the vulgar." [23]

The first college for women, Mount Holyoke College, was founded in 1837 by Mary Lyon. Although Mary Lyon was far ahead of her time in promoting the education of women, her preference for the role of woman to be in the home is indicated by her famous quotation: "Educate a man and you educate an individual. Educate a woman and you educate a family." [24]

When Oberlin College was founded as coeducational in 1833, the girls followed a separate curriculum with fewer and less demanding courses. Robert Fletcher, in his *History of Oberlin College to the Civil War,* writes: "Oberlin's attitude was that women's high calling was to be the mothers of the race, and that they should stay within that special sphere in order that future generations should not suffer from the want of devoted and undistracted mother care. If women became lawyers, ministers, physicians, lecturers, politicians or any sort of 'public character' the home would suffer from neglect. . . . Washing the men's clothes, caring for their rooms, serving them at table, listening to their orations, but themselves remaining respectfully silent in public assemblages, the Oberlin 'co-eds' were being prepared for intelligent motherhood and a properly subservient wifehood." [25]

It was not until the latter part of the nineteenth century that the right of women to higher education was firmly established. By that time several leading colleges for women had been established, most state universities admitted women, and gradually graduate schools were permitting women students. Between 1870 and 1890 the number of colleges admitting women almost doubled and the number of women students increased fivefold. It is probably safe to say that women's colleges would never have been founded had it not been for the widespread belief in the superiority of man.

The role of women in the nineteenth century also began to take on increased legal stature. Until that time woman had no recognized individuality in any sphere of life other than the home. Legally she was a tool of her husband, and any attempt that she might make to become a wage earner in her own right was to lose status and respect in the eyes of the community. It was generally believed that any woman who attempted to work outside of her domestic pursuits was unfit to be a wife and mother. A woman was deemed helpless without a man. The rise of the feminist movement began in the early part of the nineteenth century as a part of the abolitionist movement, developing into a revolt against the domesticity of women and consequently was not a popular movement in an age that held high the ideal that women belong in the home. Religion was a chief bulwark against feminine equality. The first major book by an American feminist, Sarah Grimké's *Letters on the Equality of the Sexes and the Condition of Women* (1838), attacked clergymen who insisted that God had decreed woman's domestic and inferior status as part of the divine order. During that same period Abby Kelly had so irritated people with her antislavery speeches that one New England clergyman denounced her in a sermon by using the text: "I have a few things against thee, because thou sufferest that woman Jezebel, which calleth herself a prophetess, to teach, and to seduce my servants to commit fornication" (Revelation 2:20).

To be sure, there had been women in earlier colonial days who had sought better recognition for women. Mistress Margaret Brent traveled in 1646 to Maryland, where she asked for "place and voyce" in the assembly. She was refused both. In 1776 Abigail Adams wrote to her husband, John Adams, while he was sitting in the Continental Congress: "I long to hear that you have declared an independence and, by the way, in the new code of laws, which I suppose it will be necessary for you to make, I desire you would remember the ladies and be more generous and favorable to them than were your ancestors. Do not put such unlimited power into the hands of husbands. Remember all men would be tyrants if they could. If particular care and attention are not paid to the ladies we are determined to foment a rebellion and will not hold ourselves bound to obey any laws in which we have no voice or representation." [26]

The real thrust of the feminist movement did not get under way until the middle of the nineteenth century. In 1845 Margaret Fuller published *Woman in the Nineteenth Century,* in which she argued: "What woman needs is not as a woman to act or rule, but as a nature to grow, as an intellect to discern, as a soul to live freely and unimpeded, to unfold such powers as were given her when we left our common home." [27]

During that same period Susan B. Anthony, who had taken seriously her Quaker teaching that man and woman are equal, acted as a vigorous advocate for women's rights. In 1848 the first formal meeting organized specifically to promote the rights of women met at Seneca Falls, New York, in which charges brought against men included the following:

"He has made her, if married, in the eye of the law, civilly dead.

"He has taken from her all right in property, even to the wages she earns.

"He has made her morally an irresponsible being, as she can commit many crimes with impunity, provided they be done in the presence of her husband. In the covenant of marriage, she is compelled to promise obedience to her husband, he becoming to all intents and purposes her master—the law giving him power to deprive her of her liberty and to administer chastisement.

"He has so framed the laws of divorce, as to what shall be the proper causes, and, in case of separation, to whom the guardianship of the children shall be given, as to be wholly regardless of the happiness of the woman—the law in all cases going upon a false supposition of the supremacy of man, and giving all power into his hands." [28]

This convention had three major goals: separate women and their property from complete control by men; provide opportunities for higher education for women; and achieve voting and other political rights for women. A few years later at a similar convention in Philadelphia an objector shouted from the audience: "Let women first prove that they have souls; both the Church and State deny it." [29]

Women often linked their cause to that of the Negro. In 1867 feminists in New York State tried to have the word "male" deleted at the same time as the word "white" from the constitution over the objection of Horace Greeley, who believed that this was the black man's day. In this instance the Negroes won and the women lost, despite the plea of a leading feminist: "This is the hour to press women's claims; we have stood with the black man in the Constitution over half a century, and it is fitting now that the constitutional door is open that we should enter with him into the political kingdom of equality. Through all these years he has been the only decent compeer we have had. Enfranchise him, and we are left outside with lunatics, idiots and criminals for another twenty years." [30]

The clergy gave little assistance in supporting women's rights, many of them using the Bible to support slavery for Negroes and a subordinate role for women. A Presbyterian minister, F. A. Ross, wrote a book in 1857 entitled *Slavery Ordained of God,* in which he declared: "Do you say the slave is held to involuntary servitude? So is the wife. Her relation to her husband, in the immense majority of cases, is made for her, and not by her. . . . O ye wives, I know how superior you are to your husbands in many respects—not only in personal attraction . . . in grace, in refined thought. . . . Nevertheless, he has authority from God to rule over you. . . . You are bound to obey him in all things." [31]

This view of women was also in an issue of the *Presbyterian Magazine* in 1852: "Our position is that the Bible does not favor the manhood of woman—that it is opposed to the idea of a perfect equality of the sexes. . . . This authority in the human race is vested in man, as the divinely appointed head of creation." [32]

About the same time Godey's *Lady's Book,* a favorite periodical of the time, carried the following advice to a bride from a minister: "Bear always in mind your true situation and have the words of the apostle perpetually engraven on your heart. Your duty is submission. . . . Your husband is, by the laws of God and man, your superior; do not ever give him cause to remind you of it. . . . Never exert authority over him, but remembering the wayward nature of man, still act and demean yourself according to the duty of a wife. . . . Let all your enjoyment centre in your home. Let your home occupy the first place in your thoughts; for that is the only source of happiness. Let all your endeavours be directed towards the promotion of your husband's welfare. . . ." [33]

Some of the feminists took a vigorous stand against birth control, declaring that it was another way of encouraging male aggressiveness. They preferred celibacy and absolute purity and had as their motto: "Votes For Women and Purity For Men." Other feminists such as Mrs. Woodhull went to the opposite extreme and advocated free love, declaring that the double standard was hypocritical and that women should have the same freedom that had been traditionally allotted to men. Still other feminists sought to make their movement respectable, appealing to the vast majority by linking their role in the home with the desire for more freedom. Jane Addams noted that as society grew more complicated, women needed to widen their area of concern to areas outside the home in order that they could at the same time show the importance of the home atmosphere. How could they spread the word about the value of the family if they had to stay home all the time?

Julia Ward Howe made a similar point that women's emancipation should make them better mothers: "Woman is the mother of the race, the guardian of its helpless infancy, its earliest teacher, its most zealous champion. Woman is also the home-maker; upon her devolve the details which bless and beautify family life. In all true civilizations she wins man out of his natural savagery to share with her the love of off-spring, the enjoyment of true and loyal companionship." [34]

Still other feminists argued that women were clearly superior to men. Elizabeth Cady Stanton published a paper in 1891 called "The Matriarchate, or Mother-Age," in which she argued that in early times woman had been superior to man but that Christianity and in particular Protestantism had made woman inferior. One of the most remarkable women in the entire feminist movement was Charlotte Perkins Gilman, who left her husband and child to become a writer and crusader for women's rights. Her first book, *Women and Economics,* published in 1898, argued that women should earn their own living in order to attain the fullness of humanity: "Only as we live, think, feel and work outside the home, do we become humanly developed, civilized, socialized." [35] Mrs. Gilman opposed the domestication of women and argued in favor of day nurseries and central kitchens to free young mothers for work outside the home. Her later book, *The Home* (1903), argued that learning and working at a chosen occupation were as sacred to both woman and man as were eating and sleeping: "The home is the cradle of all virtues, but we are in a stage of social development where we need virtues beyond the cradle size." [36] Moreover, the need for privacy meant that everyone—including a wife—had to escape from the home for a time. Mrs. Gilman's aim was to keep the institution of marriage relatively intact but to restructure the family relationships.

The major object of most of the feminists was to secure the right to vote. Some of the feminists insisted that women were equal to men in all important respects, while others argued that women were basically different than men, although equal, and therefore had special qualifications. Isabella Hooker declared that giving women the vote would lift the atmosphere morally since women would not tolerate immorality and corruption in government. The Women's Christian Temperance Union and the General Federation of Women's Clubs took up the banner for woman suffrage. When this vote was assured, the League of Women Voters was formed and stated: "Women unite on a humanitarian basis. There is a kinship of motherhood that binds together all women of all classes. So where the home and children are concerned, women will stand side by side in spite of creed or caste. We have also learned that home does not mean house, nor children . . . it includes world-wide welfare." [37] Surely the women suffragists overestimated what the vote would achieve.

To be sure, many men were reluctant to give women the vote, including President Grover Cleveland, who opposed this movement. The President of the Aero Club of America, Henry A. Wise Wood, testified before a congressional committee about the devastating effects of woman suffrage. He said that votes for women meant ". . . the dilution with the qualities of the cow, of the qualities of the bull upon which all the herd's safety must depend." [38] Some states had adopted woman's suffrage: Wyoming, Utah, Idaho, and Colorado, but after Utah gave women the right to vote in 1896, no other state permitted it until 1910. President Theodore Roosevelt favored the right to vote for women although he was not enthusiastic about it, pointing out that in the states that had granted that privilege, women had not been able to enhance their status. President William Howard Taft was even more hesitant, feeling that those women who do vote will be those less desirable and able while the intelligent ones would stay away from the polls.

The crux of the argument favoring woman suffrage was put forth by Mary Putnam Jacobi: "No matter how well born, how intelligent, how highly educated, how virtuous, how rich, how refined, the woman of today constitutes a political class below that of every man, no matter how base born, how stupid, how ignorant, how vicious, how poverty-stricken, how brutal. The pauper in the almshouse may vote; the lady who devotes her philanthropic thought to making that almshouse habitable may not. The tramp who begs cold victuals in the kitchen may vote; the heiress who feeds him and endows universities may not. The half-civilized hordes pouring into our country through the open gates of our seaport towns, the Indians if settled in severalty, the Negro on the cotton plantation—all, now, or in a few years, have a vote. But the white woman of purest blood, and who in her own person, or that of her mother or grandmother has helped to sustain the courage of the Revolutionary War, to fight the heroic battle of abolition, and to dress the wound of the Rebellion—this woman must keep silence. The women who embrace half the education, half the virtue, and but a fraction of the illiteracy or crime of the community—remain excluded from the franchise, buried behind this dense cloud of often besotted ignorance." [39]

Space does not permit the inclusion of other leading female suffragettes, women such as Josephine Shaw Lowell, Carey Thomas, Lucy Stone, and Carrie Chapman Catt. These and many other women played a significant role in enhancing the rights of women and moving woman toward greater equality with man. By the time the Nineteenth Amendment was passed, on August 26, 1920, giving women the right to vote, the feminist movement had lost much of its original impetus. Many of the older suffragists had become extreme in their views, leading H. L. Mencken to declare: "Years ago I predicted that these suffragettes . . . would turn out to be idiots. They are now hard at work proving it." [40] The failure of the Nineteenth Amendment to give equality to women indicates how deeply entrenched is the inferior role of women in American society. For, although in theory women had the majority of voters, men continued to dominate in all areas of society.

Another significant feature of the nineteenth century that had a profound impact in forging new styles of living was the rise of industrialization and urbanization; this occurred most rapidly in the North. Both the North and South had experienced the terribly unsettling effects of the Civil War, with its rupture of family life and its disturbance of the traditional roles of the sexes. Women had to carry on work normally done by the men who went off to fight, and the death of many of these men left numbers of widows, many of whom took off for the cities to find a new and better life. A social revolution increased in intensity and eventually made the entire country ripe for industrialization and modernization.

Until the early part of the nineteenth century, virtually every article of domestic use was made by hand. The population was essentially rural. To be sure, from the earliest colonial times there had grown towns and cities where skilled artisans had offered special talents and services. Later on mills sprang up in the communities which augmented the steady movement of families to these locales to seek employment. After 1840 the economy showed a marked shift from merchant to industrial capitalism as more and more goods could be successfully produced in the factory, and many of these manufacturers were most eager to exploit cheap female and child labor. It has been estimated that roughly two-thirds to three-fourths of the total number of factory workers in the first half of the nineteenth century were women and children. Their pay was extremely poor, their working conditions abominable, and their laboring hours long. In some areas the substitution of working women for men led to the establishment of "she towns" in which the mill workers were wives and the housekeepers husbands. In most cases the one who benefitted most from women and children working was the father since he had legal control over their wages. Industrial capitalism rapidly accelerated after 1870, often with harsh mistreatment of the working classes.

THE TWENTIETH CENTURY

By the beginning of the twentieth century, capitalism had become powerful, with individuals or corporations controlling vast segments of the country's wealth. The demand for technological specialization meant that skilled individuals had to be geographically mobile, free to move where their talents were needed. The advent of capitalism with its business ethic tended to make religion and social relationships heavily dependent on wealth and property as incentives for the virtuous man. The Protestant ethic linked man's fulfillment to his success as a man of thrift and economic security. The acquisition of wealth became for many almost a sacred calling and a sign of God's approval. Yet in most respects this world of capitalism remained a man's world, which helped to perpetuate the supposed natural superiority of the male and the existence of the double standard.

In the early part of the twentieth century, industrialization and urbanization brought changes to the traditional attitudes toward marriage, the family, and the role of sex: the economic base was shifted from the family to the factory, and conditions of employment were no longer under family or even local control. America had changed from a predominantly rural society with the dominance of so-called homogeneous Puritan values to an urban-industrial society with a pluralism of values and life styles. The melting pot of the large cities challenged traditional behavior patterns as waves of immigrants poured into the cities. These immigrants brought with them their own views of sex and marriage, which soon were modified as the second generation came into conflict with other norms. All these factors meant the shrinking of home and parental influence and an increasing number of divorces and broken families. Prerogatives that had traditionally belonged to the family were transferred to other institutions of society such as school, church, and shop. Multifamily dwellings increased. A family living in a small apartment of a multiple family dwelling, with many of its members either away at work or at school for most of the day, is far different in structure and loyalty from the kinship family of three generations living in one place and carrying on common traditions. Men found that their work made them increasingly absent from home; this led to a decline in paternal authority. The percentage of working women who were married increased from 4.6 percent in 1890 to 15.2 percent in 1940. In 1890 women made up one-sixth of the working force against one-third in 1950.

There emerged in the twentieth century the beginnings of a new sexual ethic. Urbanization had given women the opportunity to be free from parental supervision and access to more casual acquaintances with men. Literature was becoming more candid about sex, and contraceptives for men were more easily accessible. The commercialization of sex debased and made commonplace what was once a sacred and private matter. The use of the automobile made access to distant persons and places relatively easy.

Studies on sexual behavior indicate that twentieth-century woman was much more emancipated than her predecessors. This trend became particularly pronounced in the 1920s. Until the end of the nineteenth century the dominant view of the "good" woman was that she was not to enjoy sex, but was to put up with it for the sake of having children and submitting to the animal desires of her husband. William Hamilton, a surgeon-general of the United States in the nineteenth century, estimated that nine-tenths of the time good women felt no pleasure whatsoever in intercourse. Any pleasure was considered sinful; better to lie still, be calm, and grit one's teeth. The husband usually supported this view, for when such calmness within marriage became irritating to him, the double standard permitted his receiving sexual excitement outside of marriage. In the twentieth century some advocates of a new sexual ethic urged a complete change in sexual patterns that would condone both female responsiveness and permissiveness. In the 1920s Judge Ben Lindsay suggested that a period of trial marriage be instituted during which time the couple could live together and either one could withdraw from the relationship without penalty. Others advocated the abolition of marriage in its present form, Dr. Margaret Daniels suggesting that society should be organized in such a way that "men and women could mate freely and be economically independent." [41] Yet this emerging sexual freedom for woman did not truly liberate her and give her dignity. She remained virtually a prisoner in a man's world.

During this period there was a large increase in the number of divorces and grounds for divorce. In some states such as Indiana, loss of affection was considered sufficient cause. The transiency of the population, the anonymity of urban life, the increase of female independence, the lack of children in many marriages, and the fragility of family structures led to a widespread failure of the family structure. Thus, as a new sexual ethic began to develop, the traditional structures of marriage and the family were seriously threatened. Even so, public opinion remained on the side of fidelity and purity, with the usual exception, to be sure, given to male indiscretion.

Although after 1920 the percentage of women who worked increased, the rate of increase was less and even a decrease in many crucial occupations. By the end of the 1960s, one-third of the working force in the United States consisted of women, yet only a minute percentage of these women held executive positions. Today the median salary for women is about 58 percent of what it is for men, and half the women who work have salaries less than $3700 per year. Only 7 percent of physicians are women. Since the 1920s women have been receiving a decreasing percentage of advanced academic degrees and faculty positions. Women now earn 40 percent of the bachelor's degrees, 33 percent of the master's degrees, and 12 percent of the doctorates; 30 percent of the graduate students are women. In 1879 women held 40 percent of the teaching positions in higher education; by 1939 the percentage had dropped to 30; and by 1964 it had dropped to 22 (10 in the prestigious colleges). Men now comprise the majority of secondary-school teachers. Men graduating from college are usually recruited for executive positions, whereas women with the same education are offered secretarial positions. There is similar discrimination against women occupying important positions in the churches, one observer noted that Roman Catholic discrimination against women is "probably worse than in most other institutions of our society." [42] Dr. Mary Daly has commented that denial of female equality in the church ". . . is a radical affirmation of (woman's) inferior position among the people of God. By this exclusion the Church is in a very real and effective way teaching that women are not fully human and conditioning people to accept this as irremediable fact." [43]

With the waning of the influence of the church and of the effectiveness of her sanctions, there inevitably has occurred a loosening of many of the moral and social ties that used to bind marriages and families together. On the positive side this trend has freed women from their inferior role, in which the church has held them. Here is a description, quite typical, of how one person's attitude toward religion and the church changed in this century:

"Because of their firm Presbyterian beliefs, my grandparents were rigorous advocates of the philosophy of self-denial. In all things they were temperate and self-controlled. They never enjoyed pleasure for the sheer love of living—they would have thought that foolish and self-indulgent. Even now they cannot understand our enjoyment of recreations such as movies, dancing, and card parties. Of stern pioneer stuff, their modes of living imposed this life of routine self-discipline upon them, and their religion preserved these ideals. Under this type of living they prospered materially and spiritually. Mighty was the wrath of the All-Powerful God if one of his flock deviated from this narrow rigid path. . . . Their attitude toward the Bible is no less firm; it is unquestionably and absolutely true.

"Our family is much more liberal. We hold proper reverence for God, but realize, through our more advanced knowledge, that many unusual events, supernatural to our grandparents, are not directly attributable to Him. This understanding of the world and nature removes many of the fears that oppressed our grandparents. Our philosophy of living in the family group is not restriction and self-denial but rather pleasure and self-expression. We never have prayers before meals because we are always in too big a hurry. No one is home in the evenings for family prayers. There are too many places to go on Sundays, or we were out too late Saturday evening; so consequently we do not always go to church." [44]

The old religious bonds that encouraged stability have been broken. This was due in large part to the failure of the church to respond creatively and affirmatively to the new situation perpetrated by the advent of industrialization and urbanization. This process of secularization was perhaps an inevitable result of these factors as they combined with the increasing skepticism of a scientifically oriented world.

For a time science was used to support the status quo. Early scientific studies upheld the need for a patriarchal type of father and a mother who centered her activities in the home. Even Sigmund Freud permitted his bias against women to overcome his scientific interests. One interpreter has summarized Freud's views on feminine psychology as follows: "The most significant of biological factors . . . is the lack of the penis, which inevitably leads to 'penis envy' in the woman. Freud considered penis envy to be a dominant theme in all feminine life, and one that inevitably causes women to feel inferior to men. These deep seated feelings of inadequacy can be compensated for only partially by giving birth to a male child. . . . The most complicated sequence of personality development that women are subject to . . . leads inevitably . . . to a less adequate superego formation than in men. This presumably is reflected in women having a poorer sense of justice and weaker social interests than men have." [45]

Freud's followers in the United States used his views to maintain male superiority. Indeed, Freud became the new villain for women to attack, for by defining women as sex objects rather than as individuals, he ushered in a whole new set of difficulties. To quote Betty Friedan: "The fact is that to Freud, even more than to the magazine editor on Madison Avenue today, women were a strange, inferior, less-than-human species. He saw them as childlike dolls, who existed in terms only of man's love, to love man and serve his needs." [46]

In the early part of the twentieth century it could still be argued by medical scientists that there was too much harm in excessive sexual activity and that the man was by nature the aggressor and the female the passive recipient. A leading American gynecologist said to a convention of doctors in 1900: "I do not believe mutual pleasure in the sexual act has any particular bearing on the happiness of life." [47] And a book, *Facts for Husband and Wife,* published by a doctor in 1925, cautioned that one should not engage in intercourse if he is even slightly intoxicated since ". . . there is great danger that the offspring will have epilepsy or be idiotic; and a strong liking for stimulants is almost sure to be transmitted." [48]

But by the middle part of this century such views were shown by scientific studies to be just plain wrong; new sociological and physiological data challenged the old assumptions. Sexual behavior, it was noted, can differ considerably from one culture and person to another, and what may be "normal" for one may not be normal for another. The social sciences had replaced supernatural religion as the guiding force in suggesting proper forms of human behavior. Values were seen to be relative to a particular culture, and by this time a mass of data had been gathered to indicate the great variety of sexual behavior in other cultures.

It seems clear that the people of the United States must develop a new rationale for sexual attitudes and behavior if they are to respond seriously to the complex social realities which confront them. Premarital sex for the young is no longer universally considered a sin. Since World War I a new and permissive attitude toward sex on the part of both men and women—especially the young—has been steadily taking shape in society. This has been due in part to the greater availability of contraceptives, especially the "pill." But sexual freedom often creates new difficulties for the woman in her present inferior role. True sexual liberation for the female can come only with drastic modifications in the traditional Western view of the role of woman in marriage, family, and society.

What of the institution of marriage? It is true that the American people have maintained a remarkable preference for marriage. Over 90 percent of the people in the United States eventually marry, and the great majority of these marriages are terminated only by death. But it could be that for many women, marriage has been acceptable because it has been the lesser of several evils. Marriage for many women has meant more freedom and less discrimination. But it has also meant drudgery and a kind of prison that chains them to an inferior and frustrating existence, which then becomes reflected in their attitude toward spouse, children, and world. The technological revolution may have succeeded in freeing woman from many of the traditional household chores, but at the same time it has given her more time to be bored with the role of housewife and mother. General dissatisfaction with marriage has led to one-half of all marriages in California now ending in divorce. Although traditionalists may be shocked at this trend, it does seriously question the continued value of the present marital pattern. A leading women's magazine recently featured an article entitled "Are We the Last Married Generation?" and suggested that other alternative arrangements may be preferable to matrimony. If this is true even only in part, what does this do to the institution of the family? Is it doomed? Even granting the need for care of the young and the importance of love and security, are there possibly other and better arrangements for achieving these goals today than the present family structure?

Sex, marriage, and the family must be re-evaluated as to their proper functions and purposes for today. Perhaps a sensible way to see what lies ahead for us is to examine the situation in Sweden, where these problems have been faced from a modern perspective.

Three

SWEDEN
AND SEX

"The Swedes are making sex dangerous—
by American standards. They are stripping
away the old taboos. Their open attitude in-
trigues many Americans and stimulates visions of a land
where magnificent blondes enjoy their sexuality, but it also
generates worry here that our young may get some Swedish
ideas in their heads." [1] Our young do have Swedish ideas
about sex in their heads. Indeed, the United States is heading
rapidly in the direction of a Swedish sexual morality. Therefore, to prepare for our own future it is important that we
understand the Swedish way.

In some respects Sweden is very much unlike the United
States. She is a small country with a little more than 8 million
people. Only 9 percent of Sweden is suitable for cultivation,
and agriculture now accounts for only 5 percent of the gross
national product. Even more different is the homogeneity of
the Swedish people. Their geographical isolation from the
rest of the world has kept them a close knit population with

common traditions and values. There are no minority groups of any sufficient numerical strength in Sweden.

Despite these important differences the similarities between Sweden and the United States are even more remarkable. Both countries have made a major transition in the past century from a rural and predominantly agricultural economy to a highly industrialized and urbanized society. This trend has seriously threatened the traditional structures of marriage and the family.

Today both countries are affluent in comparison to the rest of the world, with Sweden the richest country in Europe and its life expectancy the longest in the world. Both countries have deep religious roots, which have been severely challenged by the creeping secularism of the twentieth century. To be sure, since the sixteenth century, Sweden has had a state Lutheran Church in contrast to the American style of denominationalism. But in both cases there has been a rather strict and uncompromising attitude toward sex, which regulated the mores and laws of each country until the social upheavals of the twentieth century. Perhaps because of her small size and homogeneity, the Swedish response to recent challenges to sexual norms has come faster than in the United States. Sweden does not claim to have *the* answer to the role of sex, marriage, and the family in our day, but she does present an alternative that must be taken seriously.

The most significant factor about modern Swedish society is its pragmatic orientation. This highly organized, technological democratic country, with such outstanding accomplishments in the area of social legislation, rejects all authoritarian dogma that comes from the past, whether economic, social, moral, or religious. To a large degree Sweden is experimental in her desire to work out tentative solutions to social problems, pluralistic in her toleration of a variety of norms and behavior patterns, and democratic in her encouragement of diversity and debate in the market place of ideas. She recognizes no final answers, preferring to work out tentative solutions in a world of rapid change. This approach is summarized in a statement made in 1966 at the centennial anniversary of the founding of the bicameral Riksdag: "In Sweden democracy is not merely a form of government. It is a way of life."

Most Swedes today no longer look to the past, hoping to find meaningful answers to their moral and religious problems. The answers to moral dilemmas that made sense to an earlier time, when the church was accepted as the guardian of faith and morals, no longer have the same authority in a modern pluralistic, pragmatic society. Radical social change in the twentieth century, which has brought unprecedented prosperity to the Swedish people, has occurred not because of but in spite of the church. Swedes see the church as having retarded what they regard as the good life, and therefore no longer turn to the church for sustenance. Their search for solutions to social and moral dilemmas must somehow be found in a new understanding of man and his proper role in a modern society. Let us examine some of the major social changes which have led to a reinterpretation of the role of women, marriage, and the family. We can properly appreciate the Swedish attitude toward sex only if we see it within the larger social setting of the movement toward equality and dignity for all.

WOMEN, MARRIAGE, AND THE FAMILY

Sweden has probably made more progress than any other Western society in the treatment of woman as equal to man. Admittedly Sweden still has a long way to go, but her progress is outstanding. By reviewing the achievements that have been made, we can better understand the role of woman in Swedish society today.

In the nineteenth century, woman's position was essentially

no different than it was in the United States. Families were large, with the kinship family dominant. The legal code of 1734 stipulated that women, married or not, must have male guardians. The father had to approve his daughter's marriage, and her husband then became her legal guardian. The woman's role was in the home, and her responsibilities included producing food and clothing in the same manner as the woman on the American frontier. In the early part of the nineteenth century she was given the legal right to earn money on her own, and fifty years later given the right to own property. But married women legally remained wards of their husbands until 1921.

The process of industrialization and urbanization began to free women from traditional roles. The family became a unit of consumption rather than production, and women as well as men moved to the cities and sought employment in industry. They were not permitted to vote nor were men who lacked sufficient capital or property. Thus, female suffrage became a part of a more general movement for universal suffrage for all adults, a goal that was finally achieved in 1918–19. The Marriage Act of 1920 provided for legal and economic equality for husband and wife. Both parties now had definite responsibilities for the welfare of each other and for their children.

In recent years new social legislation has increased benefits for health and child care. In 1955 a national health-insurance program was instituted to provide care for everyone regardless of income, and special health programs were designed for mothers and children. Mothers now receive free maternity benefits including hospital costs and a sickness benefit that covers a maximum of 180 days. A basic child allowance is now paid for every child in Sweden, regardless of the income of the parents, and an additional allowance is provided for families with handicapped children and with children over sixteen years of age who are attending school. Presently a housing allowance is paid to families with children, the amount depending on the number of children, the income of the family and the size of the apartment. Kindergartens and family day nurseries are subsidized by the state as another attempt to free women from family chores and give them opportunity to obtain employment outside the home. A full widow's pension is now paid to women who have reached the age of fifty at the time of the death of their husbands, the reason being that women over fifty would find it extremely difficult to enter the labor market. This social legislation is an outcome of the modern Swedish conviction that everything possible be done to prevent social inequality, illness, disability, old age, and death from destroying the right of the individual and/or his family to have an equal opportunity with everyone else to reap the benefits of the good life.

Tremendous strides have also been made in giving women equal opportunity with men in the labor market. In 1923 the Competence Act stated the principle, although not the implementation, of equal pay in civil service for men and women. Women's rights received a setback during the early thirties, when rising unemployment led men to discriminate against women as competitors in the labor pool. The Swedish government resisted this male movement and began to develop instead a more comprehensive program of social reform which in turn led to greater social equality. The National Pensions Act of 1935 provided equal pensions for both sexes. A law passed in 1939 declared that a woman could not be dismissed from her job for betrothal or marriage, and later legislation made it possible for wives to take leaves of absence from certain occupations to remain at home and care for their children if necessary. A law in 1946 prohibited the dismissal of employees on account of pregnancy and/or childbirth. In 1947 a law provided for equal pay for men and women in the same kind of work, and in 1960 this was extended to all segments of industry. More and more women are presently entering the labor pool. In 1966 40 percent of the labor force was women. Seventy percent of the female population between the ages fourteen and seventy-four were employed although a portion of this was part time. The tendency is definitely toward full-time employment for women, especially for those who are not married.

Despite this movement toward equality, men continue to have the vast majority of the better types of employment. Most of the women are employed in public administration, with the manufacturing industry and trade following next. About 80 percent of working women prefer traditional female occupations, probably because of social expectation. It was not until 1947 that a woman became a minister in the national government, and today women have approximately 20 percent of the seats in the parliament. The political parties are led by men and have women to handle the female issues. Women account for 25 percent of the membership of unions affiliated with the Federation of Labor, but none has a woman chairman. The executive board is all male. There are a considerable number of women who are doctors, dentists, and business owners, but they are in the minority and are seldom in the power structures of these professions where the major decisions are made.

Sweden has also developed an educational system that seeks for equality of opportunity for both sexes. During the 1920s girls were admitted to the high schools, although it was not until 1927 that girls were able to enter this level of schooling on equal par with the boys. Today school regulations state that "girls should be made aware that female labour can also make considerable contributions in those sectors which are approached by technical and mathematical-scientific studies. Girls whose interests lie in this direction should be encouraged to cultivate them." [2] To be sure, the traditional prejudice favoring differences in sex roles mitigates against the blurring of distinctions, but at least the Swedes are making a concerted effort to break down old myths. If they do not wholly succeed, they do better than the United States.

The further that Swedes go in their formal education, the larger the proportion of male students. As of 1966 the proportion of females to males qualified to enter the university was 51 percent, actually enrolled was 41 percent, graduates were 37 percent, candidates for licentiate were 16 percent, and candidates for doctorate were 8 percent. Quite obviously there are many obstacles other than the traditional role of women that prevent women from continuing their education, for example, the parents' economic situation, place of domicile, the attitude of parents, but one effective way to counter this trend is the introduction of strong adult educational programs. Although this usually makes education a part-time occupation, it at least provides the opportunity for women to secure the education which they were prevented from obtaining earlier.

In order to get married, Swedes are required to have a banns certificate. The couple must state in writing that no impediment exists to their marriage, that is, that neither is already married to another person, nor suffering from certain diseases, nor that the two are close relatives. The banns are made public, and if no obstacle is noted, the couple may be married in a church or civil service. In 1908 civil marriage was made an alternative to religious marriage. In 1951 a religious ceremony no longer remained the exclusive prerogative of the state church but was permitted by other recognized sects. The minister of justice has recently recommended that marriage should be possible through registration by both parties with no ceremony necessary. However, the legal status of living together unmarried is being strengthened so that the consequences of such a liaison—for example, children—are fully protected. The Swedish way in marriage is a long betrothal, a rather low marriage rate, a high average age for marriage—24.8 for men and 22.1 for women—and a relatively high divorce rate. However, the divorce rate, about one in six marriages, is considerably lower in Sweden than it is in the United States.

The chief reason for unhappy marriages remaining intact is for the sake of the children; however, Swedes recognize that an unhappy marriage can often do more harm to the children than if there had been a divorce. Swedish law recognizes that irreconcilable differences do exist, and in such cases divorce is preferable to continued marriage. Consequently, more and more marriage counsellors are recommending that, for the sake of the children, divorce would be the best alternative for married couples who are truly unhappy with one another. Divorce is not a serious social stigma in Sweden, for Swedes recognize that, like it or not, people do change over the years and people can grow apart as well as grow together. Normally a divorce takes one year of separation, but each couple must first talk with a marriage counsellor to see if a chance exists for reconciliation. Soon all legal grounds for divorce including adultery will probably be abolished, and divorce granted on application of either or both parties, with a proper waiting period. Even now a divorce can be granted if only one partner requests it after a year-long waiting period. It is not necessary that one of the parties be proven guilty. The highest divorce rates are to be found in the urban areas, the most common reason being, as the law puts it, "deep and permanent cleavage."

"One-parent" families are becoming more prevalent in Sweden. In addition to divorced parents, widows, and widowers, there are women and some men who prefer to have children but not to marry. Both single men and women may adopt children. An increasing number of young women who have children outside of wedlock are choosing to keep their children rather than give them up for adoption. There is a general acceptance of unwed mothers by society. A recent study in Stockholm of five hundred unmarried mothers under the age of twenty indicated that a majority of them had kept their children. Children of unmarried parents normally have priority in attending day nurseries since their parents would otherwise have difficulty finding work. Studies have been made in Sweden of the differences between young children whose mothers work outside the home and those who do not. The results of these studies conflict, but the best evidence seems to indicate that the decisive factor is not whether the mother works outside the home, but whether there is a warm relationship between mother and child, whether the mother is happy with her combination of home and work, and whether the children have adequate care when the mother is not home.

The Swedes are also rethinking the proper roles of mother and father in the family relationship as a part of the desire of the female for equality. They are trying to break down the traditional idea of man as the provider and woman as the keeper of the home. To them this view perpetuates the notion of woman as inferior. In a highly industrialized and technological society this sharing of home and family responsibilities on an equal basis is becoming more and more possible. Studies have indicated that when the woman works only in the home, 12 percent of the men help with the housework. When the woman finds gainful employment, 29 percent of the men then help at home. A small number of fathers choose to remain at home to care for the children while the mother works.

There is in Sweden today a strong feminist movement that is pushing for more rapid progress toward equal rights for women and for the enhancement of woman's role in society. One such protagonist is Eva Moberg, who argues that marriage should be an equal partnership in which both parents share responsibility for work in the home and both have a profession of their choosing. She writes: "We should stop hammering in the concept of 'women's two roles.' Both men and women have *one* main role—as human beings. To care for offspring is part of the *human role* by necessity and moral duty, but also a rich asset, a delightful experience and much more." [3]

Mother love, she insists, "is history's most exploited emotion." She and other feminists argue for shorter working hours to enable husband and wife to combine more easily work within and without the home. They also opt for raising boys and girls in exactly the same way and for more collective supervision of young children. Other feminists prefer the abolition of the family structure. Barbro Backberger has argued that the typical kinship family is a remnant of an outmoded society, that "pathological monogamy" is considered sacrosanct while other styles of living more amenable to today's society are condemned as immoral. She advocates any and all kinds of living relationships among consenting adults as long as the rights of children are protected. There are in Stockholm and other large cities some instances of "megafamilies"—groups of unrelated adults and their children—living together, although these are not nearly as prevalent in Sweden as they are in Denmark.

However, most feminists prefer to work within the present structure of marriage and the family. Their primary goal is a society that gives equal rights to women, a society which acknowledges that the first responsibility of both women and men is to be a human being. Alva Myrdal, a member of the present Swedish cabinet and one of the most respected women in Sweden today, affirms this goal:

When wives of today—considering their long life expectancy and their small families—can no longer bury their individuality under the role of "housewives," their development as individuals will come more and more to the forefront. Their opportunities for using more years in outside employment will fortify this trend towards a more independent role, as 30–40 years of active life remain to them even after a "motherhood service period," and the realization that in our societies there is a likelihood of women having to live alone as widows for a considerable number of years —six is the average in Sweden—will further strengthen the necessity for women to look upon their own life as an individual destiny. Needless to say, this will have important successive effects on the children—their conception of what mothers and women are—and ought to be—will be changed accordingly. But for people who are responsible in practice for education and social policy, there can be no virtue in idly waiting for the effects to work themselves out. Society—from vocational schools to taxation laws —as well as the coming generation of women and men, must start to visualize more clearly what kind of world we are heading for. That world is one where the role and status of women will—or could—be greatly enhanced, and where their functions will not, as still is the case, be predominantly cut out to be the servants of others.[4]

SWEDEN AND SEXUAL BEHAVIOR

The gradual breakdown in the double standard between man and woman has had definite implications in the area of sexual attitudes and behavior. What is true for one sex must also be true for the other. If virginity is not necessarily a virtue for unmarried men, then it is also not necessarily a virtue for unmarried women. One book, *Ways to Maturity,* puts it this way: "In countries where it is generally believed that a woman has no right to sexual experience prior to marriage, it is deemed especially important that the hymen be intact on the wedding night to prove that the bride has been previously untouched. . . . Here in Sweden, on the other hand, the view that women and men have the same right to sexual experience is becoming more and more common."[5]

To those who still try to defend a double standard on the biological ground that it is the woman who gets pregnant, the Swedes reply that with present methods of birth control now reliable and easily available, pregnancy can be avoided. Moreover, the risk of a potential tragedy arising from an unwanted pregnancy is as great within marriage as without. The point is that the risk can be minimized, and therefore, the "pregnancy argument" is no longer valid. Equality between the sexes means equality in sexual behavior.

The fact that Sweden is rather permissive in her sexual attitudes and behavior is due in large part to this breakdown of the double standard. Recent studies indicate that about 80 percent of boys and 65 percent of girls have had sexual relations by the age of eighteen, and the percentage is increasing steadily. In two studies of the sex habits of college students, in 1960 and 1965, conducted by Professor George Karlsson, then of Uppsala and now of Umeå University, the percentage of male students who had experienced intercourse increased from 72 to 81 and the percentage of girls from 40 to 65. Perhaps more significant was the increase for males at church-related schools: from 38 percent to 77 percent. Other studies indicate that the sex habits of Swedish college students are virtually the same as those of noncollege young people.

Another study in the city of Örebrö indicated that intercourse had been experienced by 57 percent of the boys, with the median age for first intercourse sixteen. For the girls 46 percent had had intercourse, with the median age for first intercourse seventeen. Eighty-three percent of the boys and 38 percent of the girls had masturbated, with the beginning age for boys, 13.3, and girls, 12.8. This particular study also probed the reasons these individuals had for engaging in their first intercourse experience. The overwhelming majority of both sexes gave as the reason for first intercourse that they themselves wanted it. Not a single boy or girl acquiesced because his or her partner threatened to break off the relationship. In fact, this study seemed to indicate that when the girl is treated as equal to the boy, there is less chance that either party will treat sex casually or acquiesce merely to conform.

Over 80 percent of engaged couples have sexual relationships. It should be pointed out that in rural Swedish society there has been a strong tradition that the man impregnates his fiancée before the marriage to make sure that she can bear children and thus perpetuate the farm. For this reason children were an economic necessity, and the tradition, tacitly approved by the church, is deeply imbedded in Swedish customs. A similar tradition is found in Denmark, where betrothal was considered the essential agreement and the wedding ceremony often delayed until a convenient time, which was often after the birth of the first child. In both Sweden and Denmark this custom has been rationalized and continued in urban society. The reason most often used today is that the severe housing shortage delays marriages.

The residents of the Danish island of Bornhold also had an old custom called "lying in the Christmas hay." On Christmas Eve all the farmhouse beds were made with fresh linen and left for the dead who were believed to visit their former homes for the next two weeks. The farm residents would then sleep together for that period in a bed of hay, their version of group sex. Today in urban centers such as Copenhagen, groups of couples gather together for communal sex sessions. The norm of such groups is that to have group sex together is permissible, but that sex in private should occur only with one's regular partner.

Another study of premarital sexual behavior in Sweden was done in 1967 in Stockholm covering the age group sixteen to twenty-five. This study embraced 2,600 young people, and special emphasis was placed on probing the reasons for the initiation of sexual intercourse. The results indicated that petting almost always led to sexual intercourse, and that only 3 of the 2,600 interviewed delayed sexual experience until marriage. The average age for first intercourse was sixteen for boys and seventeen for girls. Social background and educational experience had little to do with sexual behavior.

Seventy-three percent of the males and 81 percent of the girls said that women should have sexual experience before marriage, and only 20 percent of the men and 13 percent of the women still believed in the double standard in sex. About 20 percent of those interviewed used contraceptives at first intercourse, with half of them using condoms. Thirty percent of the men and 39 percent of the women had had two to six sexual partners.

There is no general public stigma in Sweden against engaging in premarital sex. It is assumed by Swedish society—90 percent, according to one study—that engaged couples are having intercourse. Another study in 1955 indicates that although 80 percent of those interviewed disapproved of premarital sex that was not a "prelude to marriage," only 14 percent disapproved in 1970. The typical advice of a Swedish mother to her teenage daughter would not be: "Don't do it!" but rather "Be careful when you do." *So far all studies indicate that premarital sex does not lead to extramarital sex.* Over 90 percent of married couples believe in fidelity within the marriage covenant, which is probably a larger percentage than in the United States. In a poll taken several years ago, 94 percent of married partners declared that "fidelity was among the most important values in a marriage"; only 3 percent declared fidelity unimportant. Permissive premarital sexual experience does not seem to affect the stability of future marital and family relationships.

The State Commission for Sex Education in 1969 made a thorough study on "Sex Life in Sweden." The results give a broad preview of sexual attitudes and behavior among a representative sample of the total Swedish population between eighteen and sixty years of age. Ninety-five percent of this entire group had had sexual intercourse, with the median age for first intercourse 17.5. This median age for first intercourse had decreased by one year between 1920 and the present study. Eighty-five percent of the entire group believed that "being in love" was a valid reason for premarital intercourse. Fifty-four percent favored premarital sexual intercourse for women and 62 percent for men. Ninety percent asserted that fidelity in marriage was absolutely essential, and the same percentage reported remaining faithful in their marriage. Eighteen percent of married men and 45 percent of married women declared that their present marriage partners had been their only sexual contact. When they were asked about the number of sexual partners within the last month, 87 percent reported one partner, 6 percent two, 4 percent three to five, and 2 percent more than five.

Seventy-one percent of the entire group believed that use of birth control was absolutely essential at each intercourse when couples did not seek conception. Yet 27 percent declared that on their last intercourse they did not take due precautions even though conception was not desired. There was a positive correlation between "sexual conservatism" and rural residence, female sex, lower income, less education, and regular church attendance. Eighty-six percent of the entire group favored sex education in the school, and 89 percent believed that young people should be taught the use of contraceptives.[6]

Sex Education

Sweden has had sex education in the public schools since 1944, and this education has been compulsory since 1956. The Swedes would admit that, ideally speaking, it is preferable for most children to receive their sex education at home. But they also know that such education has not been forthcoming and, moreover, that many parents are ill-equipped to deal with such a sensitive subject. Therefore, the schools must assume this important responsibility. The charge is often made that Swedish sex education is purely factual and lacks a moral basis. Such a charge has no basis in fact, although the

Swedes would be the first to admit that in a pluralistic pragmatic society no one specific pattern of sexual behavior can
be normative for everyone. The *Handbook on Sex Instruction
in Swedish Schools* has the following statement of purpose:

The purpose of sex instruction in Swedish schools is to give
biological information and to impart knowledge in a manner that
will help both in the moulding of ideals and in the building of
character. Instruction on these lines is intended to have a pronounced ethical basis.

[This handbook includes such statements as the following:]
There is no other field in which it is so important to emphasize
that the school's task is not only to give information but also to
train character. If there is one aspect of living which cannot be
divorced from character and conscience it is sex. Since an individual's experiences of sex can leave deep traces on his character, for
good or evil, it is most important that an educator should con-
tinually bear in mind the intimate effect of sex on the formation
of ideals and moral attitudes.

The danger of separating sexual desire from love should be
stated, and the fact that sex can never give any real satisfaction
without an emotional attachment towards the partner, whereas sex
combined with communion of spirit bestows lasting happiness.
Young people must be taught to understand that those who do
not live in accordance with these precepts run great risks.[7]

The organization primarily responsible for the introduction
of sex education in the schools is the Swedish Association for
Sex Education, better known as RFSU (Riksförbundet för
Sexuell Upplysning). RFSU was founded in 1933 primarily
through the efforts of Elise Ottesen-Jensen, Sweden's most
outstanding pioneer in making birth control information
available to the public. This organization has been responsible
for many of the sex reforms of the past three decades and has
been largely self-supporting through its sale of contraceptives.
Its general aims are directed toward "harmonious sexual
relations and planned parenthood, greater candor and in-

creased knowledge in sexual matters; reduced prejudice and greater tolerance in regard to sexual morality and sexual behavior; expanded research and broader information about biological, psychological, social, and cultural aspects of sex life; improved conditions for families and single parents; increased Swedish contributions to international planned parenthood projects." [8]

Sex education is not taught as a separate course but, rather, introduced wherever appropriate in biology, civics, and religion. The rationale for this approach is that sex should be treated as a normal dimension of man's personhood and incorporated as naturally as possible in the study of man. This study begins with the first grade and continues through the equivalent of high school. Sex education becomes more extensive and intensive with each passing year, reaching its high point perhaps in the ninth grade. Here, for example, is a typical lesson at the elementary level:

Your home hasn't always been there. Mummy and Daddy like each other very very much, and so they wanted to spend all their lives together in their own home. They got a place to live in and bought some tables and chairs and a lot of other things. But a home isn't a real home if there aren't any children, and they did so want to have some children. And where did the children come from? Well, perhaps you know that already. They came from Mummy's body. I'm going to tell you a little more now about where a little child comes from.

Inside Mummy's body there are a lot of eggs, not big ones like a hen's but little ones—ever so tiny, tinier than a pin's head. They haven't got a shell on them, only a thin skin. They have a special home in a little room in Mummy's body. One day one of the eggs starts to grow. Soon there is a little head, and little arms and legs. If you could see the little creature in the special little room in Mummy's abdomen you would know that it was a baby growing there. It gets food from its Mummy through a tube which goes into its abdomen. It grows and grows, but it takes a long time.

For nine whole months the baby lies in Mummy's body. As the child grows inside, Mummy changes too. Her abdomen becomes bigger, and Mummy finds her baby heavy to carry around. But, after nine months, it has become so big that there isn't any more room for it. One day Mummy feels a pain, and then she and Daddy know that the baby is going to be born. It can be born at home or in a maternity hospital. Then the baby comes out through the opening between Mummy's legs. The opening becomes bigger when the child is going to be born, then it closes up again. The midwife, who helps when the baby is being born, cuts the tube through which it got its food when it was in Mummy's body. And as a reminder of the tube we all have a little mark on our abdomens. We call it our navel. After the baby has been born Mummy needs a few days' rest.

Mummy and Daddy wait eagerly to find out whether the baby is a boy or a girl. If it is a girl she has a little opening between her legs like her Mummy. Boys don't have an opening between their legs; instead they have something about as big as a finger and called a penis.

When the baby has been born everybody is very glad to hear it cry for the first time. That means it is alive and has begun to breathe, and it is soon able to take food in through its mouth. But it still gets food from its Mummy, only now it gets it by sucking milk from her breast. We say that the baby sucks and that the mother feeds or nurses her child.

Now I have told you how a baby comes into the world. There is only one thing I haven't told you, and that is a very important one. It is this: How can the little egg in Mummy's body suddenly begin to grow? It can't just do it all by itself. To explain how it happens we must first talk a little about Daddy.

Inside Daddy's body there are some small seeds called sperms. They are even smaller than the eggs that Mummy has. But they are necessary for the egg to begin to grow. A sperm from Daddy and an egg from Mummy grow together, and that is how a baby comes about.

That is why a child is like both its Mummy and its Daddy. Perhaps it isn't so easy to recognize when you are little, but it usually becomes clearer and clearer the bigger you grow.

Parents have longed for a child, and are so happy when it has come into the world. Mummy and Daddy have to help it and look after it in every way they can. For, you know, it's a long long time before the child can really look after itself.[9]

In grades 4 through 6 (ages eleven through thirteen) students are taught the differences between the sexes, the structure and function of the sexual organs, puberty, menstruation, wet dreams, masturbation, conception, development of the fetus and pregnancy, labor, etc. In an examination of this material students might be asked such questions as the following:

1. What is meant by masturbation?
2. Name some of the changes in a boy when he reaches puberty.
3. What changes occur in girls at about the same age?
4. What is meant by intercourse?
5. When does actual fertilization take place?
6. Why are contraceptive techniques sometimes used?

In grades 7 through 9 (ages fourteen through sixteen) the instruction is given in more detail and also includes information on spontaneous and induced abortions, venereal diseases, sterilization, sexual abnormalities, and proper use of contraceptives. In the ninth grade there are visits to birth-control centers, and each student that year is expected to have a minimum of ten hours of practice in child care: feeding and bathing an infant, changing diapers, etc. A typical examination might include the following questions:

1. What is a condom?
2. What is a cervical diaphragm?
3. What three contraceptive techniques are safest?
4. What contraceptive technique is best for teenagers and why?
5. Why do you think the number of unmarried teenagers having children is increasing?

One ninth-grade biology text has the following to say about contraceptives: "There are contraceptives for both men and women. The one used most often is called a condom, and it is used by the man. It is not a reliable safeguard against impregnation because a condom can very easily break. It is considerably safer for a woman to use a vaginal diaphragm. This is a rubber bowl that covers the mouth of the uterus. Fitting of a vaginal diaphragm must be done by a physician. However, there is no 100 percent protection against impregnation. Many people have learned this through bitter experience after entering sexual relationships. Nor do contraceptives protect against venereal disease. Since young boys and girls should not have sexual contacts, they should not use contraceptives either." [10]

Frankness and openness are encouraged, and questions are answered in a straight-forward way. For example, here is what one teacher has reported as typical questions asked by seventh graders: "Is having intercourse fun? How does it feel? Does it feel the same for girls as for boys? Does it hurt very much the first time? [this from a girl] Does something come out of the girl too? Does it hurt having children? Does it hurt so much that even grown women cry? When do you think we should have intercourse for the first time? My opening is so small, will I be able to have intercourse? How can a boy put his penis into a girl, it looks so soft. [And after the answer to this question:] But what if it isn't erect just when one wants to have intercourse? Can a woman have children without intercourse? Do old women [she probably meant forty-year-olds] also like to have intercourse? Do you have to show your naked body for the boy you sleep with?" [11]

Although such straight-forward honesty in discussing such questions may be shocking to some individuals, it should also be emphasized that moral considerations are discussed with equal concern and frankness. Here, for example, is a lesson for ages fourteen to sixteen:

Young people and old people—all have their special problems which they must try and solve. At your age there are several things to wonder about. Much has happened to you recently. You aren't children any longer as you were before, but you aren't really adults either, though sometimes you would rather like to think so. When you were smaller you didn't need to take responsibility for your actions in the same way as you do now. It is very important that you should soon learn to accept this responsibility. The reason is that at your age you are meeting with things which other people cannot take responsibility for in the same way. This is particularly true of relations between the sexes. During your earlier years at school you were all playmates, boys and girls together—even if you did not always agree too well. It is different now. Interest in the opposite sex has awakened. A boy and a girl find perhaps that they get on particularly well together. They are happier in each other's company than in anyone else's. Before long they feel that the thing that draws them to each other is more important for them than anything else which has ever happened to them. That feeling of being alone with one's problems vanishes. The feeling of having something in common with another human being, the feeling that someone really understands you and longs to be near you—all this transforms your whole being and your whole outlook on humanity and existence. Love between two people is a mighty force, which can draw forth the best from them. It makes them want to do fine things. You want to give your very best to the one you love, you want the one you care for to feel secure and happy.

To succeed in these efforts you must of course try and understand the feelings of the one you love and not only think of yourself and your own feelings. It might be well to stop a moment and consider this. Boys and girls of your age don't dream about the future in quite the same way. You who care for one another should think of that. Girls may at first think about engagement, marriage and the home they would like to set up later on. Boys too think thoughts like these when they are a little older. They think about what they are going to be, about training for the career they think of choosing, and such like. Sooner as a rule than girls they long to possess completely the one they love. Perhaps they want to begin having a sexual life together straight away, although that is something that ought only to belong to the lives of adults. Now if a boy really wants a girl to feel secure and happy with him he must show her every consideration. He should not upset the way in which she is developing. If he tries to force her to do something for which she is not ready and about which she feels unhappy there is a serious risk that she will get a twisted attitude to the whole of sex and love.

At your age, and in general while you are still growing up, you should not engage in sexual relations. As I am sure you can see, two people ought not to begin an intimate sexual life with one another before they are in a proper position to take responsibility for any children who may be born and to care for them and give them a good home to come to. Don't imagine that you can rely on contraceptives to prevent pregnancy and children being born. Nor are there any other absolutely sure methods against that possibility. Boys are very ready to assure girls that nothing of that sort can happen. But it happens sometimes all the same.

It must also be borne in mind that a girl who becomes pregnant before she is fully adult has to pass through a hard time before the child is born and an even harder time afterwards, when she is certain to lack the support and help she needs. Instead of looking forward to having the child she is afraid of the future. She is not ready for such a trial.

If you think more carefully about what is best for the one you love, for the child and for yourself, then you ought to be led to live a life of continence during the years while you are growing up.

The essential meaning and purpose of sexual relations is that it should lead to the birth of children. But you should also know that intercourse is in itself a rich source of happiness for those who experience it in the right circumstances.

Now it is often not so easy for boys and girls to lead continent lives during the years of growth. A girl should remember not to make it harder through her own behavior—through letting a boy enter too intimately into her life—for herself and for him to resist the instinctual urge. Boys' resistance is usually less than girls'.

This means that boys have all the more responsibility and must try to exert their self-control. Girls must "hold themselves back," and boys must learn to understand how valuable this is.

One thing that makes it difficult for many young people to abstain from sexual relations is the bad example of their friends. There are many perhaps who see that they ought to abstain, but then they see that a lot of their friends don't trouble about this at all. It can happen that girls who hold themselves back think that they won't be liked as much as the others. There is something wrong about a group of young people in which this is true. Most boys have more respect for girls who hold themselves back, and those girls are indeed worthy of that respect. It is essential for you young people to appreciate that those who have the intelligence and will-power to avoid sexual relations during the years when they are growing up have the best prospects later in life for sexual happiness and a fortunate experience of love. You must also remember that it is not very often that the one about whom you first dream fond dreams will also be the one at whose side you will live the whole of your life.

There is much that seems designed to undermine resistance not least for young people. I especially wish to draw your attention to the way alcoholic drinks reduce the ability to reflect and blunt the power to make judgments. Dancing in particular, in conjunction with the drinking of wine or spirits, has a sexually exciting effect, and experience shows that these two things together often lead to sexual relations. There are many people who find themselves behaving in a way they come to regret bitterly. Loose and casual sexual relations are often formed like this under the influence of drink. Experience also shows that a considerable amount of venereal infection occurs in association with intoxication.

By abstaining from sexual relations during the years when you are still growing up, you are giving yourself the best prospects for one day building your own home with the one you love, and living happily together.[12]

In the equivalent of our high school (ages seventeen through twenty), instruction becomes even more detailed and also includes such issues as welfare measures during pregnancy and after birth, the options for unwed pregnant women, legal and moral responsibilities for both mother and father to a child born out of wedlock, moral aspects of sex, etc.

At present there is a controversy going on in Sweden concerning the precise responsibility that the schools should assume in teaching the moral dimension to sexual relationships. What kinds of sexual behavior should be encouraged and what kinds discouraged? Heretofore, as the preceding quotation indicates, the schools have tried to teach that the ideal is to confine sexual intercourse to the marriage covenant. The former Handbook stated: "The teacher must uphold the view that continence during adolescence is the only course the school can recommend with a good conscience. It gives the individual the best prospects for happiness later on." [13]

However, this ideal is not confirmed by current practice, and modern reformers are urging that this present bias in favor of premarital chastity be omitted from the instructions. Thus the latest version of the Handbook reads: "It is important for the students to realize that laws and norms vary from time to time, from people to people, and that within one and the same country, different groups may have different views on sex relations; also that the norms of one culture cannot be directly transferred to another culture. However, the fact that norms are relative should not be taken as implying that no norms are required. As a social being, man must respect the demands of society in his sexual behavior as elsewhere." [14]

The Swedes recognize that their sex education program is far from perfect, and a Royal Commission is now at work revising the program. One criticism is that many older people would prefer that a definite sexual norm of abstinence outside of marriage continue to be taught. A few years ago, 140 Swedish physicians joined in a statement that criticized the present sex education program and urged that "firmer sexual norms" be stressed. About the same time a similar statement from 200,000 "Christian women" made the same point. A recent, thorough study of the attitudes of Swedish people ages eighteen to sixty revealed the following concerning what the schools should teach:[15]

	Age 18–23	Age 24–60
Teach abstinence	4%	20%
Teach all attitudes, recommend abstinence	33%	47%
Teach all attitudes, leave conclusions to students	60%	31%
Teach all attitudes, recommend "freedom"	3%	2%

A national organization of Swedish high school students has complained that sex education is often too moralistic, and they have argued that only factual data about sex be taught. Their position is vigorously supported by RFSU, which considers many of the just-quoted statements from the Handbook as moralistic, and out of touch with prevailing youth norms and accurate scientific and sociological information. It is clear that Sweden has not yet solved the problem of the most effective kind of sex education. The Swedes made sex education compulsory for the students without making it compulsory for the instructors. Many of the teachers are middle-aged and older and a number of them have their own hang-ups and embarrassments in talking about sex. It is not uncommon for poor instructors to limit sex education to a few slides and to prohibit or at least curtail discussion. In fairness to the teachers it should be pointed out that only a minority of them consider themselves sufficiently trained to teach sex education. This poor quality of instruction may be why, despite the fact that sex education is compulsory, only about a half of the young people receive an adequate sex education. The Swedish Board of Education never has stated how many hours should be devoted to sex education, the amount varying radically from school to school. A recent study of ninth-graders indicated that 93 percent of the entire group had been taught sex information in biology, 42 percent in civics, and 53 percent in religion. Eighty-three percent reported that they had received information about contraception, and 82 percent wanted more teaching than they had received.

Dr. Bergström-Walan has written of the quality of teaching: "Sex education in schools is mostly handled by teachers who lack the necessary training. These teachers usually fit into one of the following three categories: those who feel compelled to teach the course out of a strong sense of duty, those who are interested and take a healthy approach to the subject, and those who are interested but are misdirected and get an unhealthy pleasure out of seeing and hearing young people try to explain their thoughts about sex, their experiences and worries." [16]

Parallel with sex education has come an increasing incidence of gonorrhea and unwanted pregnancies. The Swedes are quick to deny that this has any necessarily direct cause-effect relationship with sex education, pointing to other factors such as improved statistics and the emerging sexual freedom of woman, who often affirms her new sexual freedom by misusing it, urbanization, technology, etc. Undoubtedly these are important factors. The Swedes are among the most statistic-minded people in the world. And because unmarried mothers have attained a high degree of social acceptability, there is less care with the proper use of contraceptives. Still one would hope that sex education could be more effective in curtailing unfortunate consequences of the misuse of sex. Although one cannot expect such a program to curtail all undesirable consequences any more than religion can eliminate sin, there should be more successful methods of solving these serious social problems.

By and large, however, the Swedish people are firmly committed to a program of compulsory sex education in the public schools. There has never been a question of its possible discontinuation. The question that is being faced is how this program can be improved. This is the task that has been undertaken by the Royal Commission.

OTHER TRENDS IN SWEDEN

Four other trends stand out which also reflect the Swedish attitude toward sex that has become dominant in recent years. The first of these is the availability of birth control information and devices. Until 1938 it was illegal to provide knowledge about contraception, but since that date the Swedish government has taken an increasingly active role in the dissemination of such information. Diaphragms and the "pill" are available to almost every woman over the age of fifteen. Maternal health clinics are now required to give contraceptive advice to both married and unmarried women, and free contraceptives are available to married women who cannot afford them. Mail-order houses advertise widely in the newspapers and magazines concerning the purchase of birth control devices, RFSU being the largest seller. Male contraceptives can be purchased in automats along the streets of the larger cities, a practice approved by the Archbishop of the Church of Sweden as a means of preventing the spread of venereal disease. The Swedish news media and billboards are filled with advertisements recommending birth control. One can often spot billboards showing a beautiful Swedish blonde girl and a handsome young man looking eagerly into each other's eyes, with the caption printed underneath: "Babies? Yes—but when we want them" or "Both of you are responsible. Can she depend on you? Can you depend on yourself? . . . to be safe is the most important thing." The Swedish rationale for a strong birth control program is that it is better to have fewer unwanted children even at the risk of increased sexual activity. However, some Swedes insist that greater knowledge and availability of contraceptives does not necessarily imply greater sexual license. As one Swedish child psychologist puts it: "It is the ignorant youngsters who get into trouble: when they are exposed to primitive impulses and passions, they just don't know how to cope with them. Knowledge doesn't mean temptation. The young people who are getting a decent sex education are becoming much more sure of themselves. They are developing stronger egos so that they can handle their sex drives in a more mature, rational way." [17]

A second trend is the increasing ease with which abortions can be obtained. Under the present law of 1938, which has been amended several times—most recently in 1963—an abortion may be obtained if:

1. childbirth would entail serious danger to the life or health of a woman suffering from illness, a physical defect, or weakness as indicated by medical and medico-social authorities.

2. there is reason to assume that childbirth and child care would seriously damage a woman's physical or psychic strength in view of her living conditions and other special circumstances.

3. a woman has become pregnant as a result of rape, other criminal coercion, or incestual sexual intercourse, or if she is mentally retarded, legally insane, or under fifteen years of age at the time of impregnation.

4. there is reason to assume that either parent of the expected child might transmit to the offspring hereditary insanity, imbecility, serious disease, or a serious physical handicap.

5. there is reason to assume that the expected child will suffer from serious disease or deformity resulting from injury during fetal life.[18]

Interruption of pregnancy for other than disease or a physical defect may not occur after the twentieth week of pregnancy. Abortions may be authorized by the National Board of Health and Welfare, by two doctors, or by one doctor in certain emergency situations where a woman's life is in danger. The law allows considerable flexibility of interpretation. Even so, there is now a movement underway to liberalize further the laws, and it seems likely that soon an abortion can be obtained solely if the woman asks for it.

A law of 1941 authorizes the National Board of Health to authorize sterilization: (1) if there is reason to assume that the subject would transmit mental disease, imbecility or another serious disease or physical handicap to his children; (2) because of mental derangement or a social way of life the individual is unable to assume responsibility for the proper rearing of children; (3) if pregnancy would entail serious danger to a woman's life or health.[19] Sterilization as a means of birth control is not widely used or recommended in Sweden.

A third trend is the lack of censorship and the removal of virtually all restrictions on pornography. "Sex Shops" containing so-called pornographic material are to be found in the larger cities in both Sweden and Denmark. At present the Danes have two restrictions on pornography: first, such pictures cannot be sold or distributed to children under sixteen years of age; second, there can be no public window displays of such pictures. The Swedes have the former restriction, but not the latter. However, the law will probably soon be changed to conform with the Danish law. The only restriction on movies is one of age. Children under sixteen years of age are not permitted to attend movies containing a high degree of sex or violence, and the latter category includes many Hollywood-made movies.

The Swedish and Danish conviction is that what constitutes pornography is largely a matter of taste, and the government should not attempt to dictate the tastes of adults. These countries admit that the age-sixteen limitation is purely arbitrary and that there is as yet no convincing evidence that children are in any way damaged by what some adults consider to be pornographic material. However, there is no concerted movement in either country to lower the age. It seems significant that since the recent removal of restrictions on so-called pornographic material in Denmark, the sale of such material has dropped considerably. As one editor of such material put it: "The game is not what it used to be. The days of specialization in pornography have gone. I think that in the future pornography will be judged on a quality standard, just like all other films and books." [20] An indication of the same trend in Sweden can be noted in the publication of four volumes of erotic short stories entitled *Love 1*, *Love 2*, *Love 3*, and *Love 4*. The first two volumes sold 300,000 copies within the early months of publication. The other two have had considerably fewer sales, and so have other similar books. To be sure, both Sweden and Denmark are signatories to the International Postal agreement, which prohibits use of the mails to distribute so-called pornographic material.

A final trend that we shall mention is the liberalization of the laws regulating sexual relationships. The Swedish tradition, following the preference of the state church, was to limit sexual relations to the marriage relationship. However, as we have already noted, the church was forced eventually to give tacit acceptance to a sexual relationship between the betrothed. Until the twentieth century legislation was framed according to the wishes of the Lutheran Church. In this century the trend has been in the direction of permitting any kind of sexual relationship between consenting adults in private, that sex is essentially a private matter and not subject to public control except in the case of aggressive behavior.

The Criminal Code of 1962 prohibits intercourse between a person and his or her own child or its offspring and between siblings. However, liberal elements are arguing that the crime of incest should be abolished and that protection of young persons against sexual abuse should be the same whether or not the offender is a relative. One interesting recent case concerns two couples of half-siblings who were convicted of having sexual relations. One of the couples continued living together and a child was born. Although this was clearly a breach of the Criminal Code of 1962, the government in 1969 decided to drop the case.

The laws concerning homosexual relationships have also been liberalized. In 1944 a reform bill was passed which abolished the idea of "unnatural offenses" between members of the same sex. However, there was concern that homosexual acts with children could impair their development, and, therefore, the age barrier against sexual relations with young people was kept at eighteen, three years above the limit for heterosexual relations. In 1969 the minister of justice suggested that the age restriction be the same for both homosexual and heterosexual acts. With respect to rape, until 1965 it was considered a violent crime that could take place only outside of marriage. In 1965 the government accepted the view that rape was a crime whether it occurred within or outside of marriage.

The Criminal Code of 1864 made the age fifteen as the limit to give children protection against sexual relationships, and offenses against children under the age of twelve made the penalty even more severe. In the Criminal Code of 1962 the general age limit is still fifteen, but the prosecutor usually drops the case if the offenders are both about the same age. This code also contained a provision that an attempt to obtain sexual relations with a person under eighteen years of age by giving economic compensation should be considered an offense as a means of combatting juvenile crime. However, this law has never been strictly enforced and will probably soon be eliminated. The major principle for protection of young people is that heterosexual and homosexual acts should be treated the same way, with the only difference being one of age. Where the limit is fifteen for heterosexual acts, it is eighteen for homosexual ones.

Since 1918 prostitution in itself has not been considered a

crime. The laws against prostitution are attempts to prevent young people from becoming prostitutes and to punish those persons who exploit others. Prostitution still exists in Sweden, but is far less rampant than in countries which have more restrictive sex laws and a double moral standard. There are very few sex crimes as such—primarily rape and abuse—but these offenses are not always easy to prove in court. As mentioned earlier, venereal diseases are on the increase. However, there is no shame attached to venereal diseases as patients are treated free of charge, and VD is listed along with the other communicable diseases such as tuberculosis and small pox. The reason is that it is as immoral to expose a person to small pox as it is to venereal disease. Thus, the Swedes are remedial rather than punitive toward individuals who have sexual problems or who break the sex laws. They seek to respect the dignity, welfare, and privacy of the individual.

The Role of the Church in Modern Sweden

To appreciate the role of the church in modern Sweden, we need to understand the historical development of the church and the prominent role she has played in the past. Christianity had its origins in Scandinavia in the ninth century, and in the subsequent centuries missionaries from the Continent traveled to the northwest to "convert the heathen." Newly converted vikings would also return from the battlefields carrying the torch for Christ. Norway and Denmark were "christianized" in the eleventh century, with Sweden following shortly thereafter. In 1104 a bishopric was established in Lund, and in 1164 one in Uppsala, thus setting the stage for a rivalry which has continued to the present day.

Roman Catholicism was the dominant religion until Gustav Vasa appointed himself head of the national church at about the time of his coronation in 1523. In 1536 a church assembly at Uppsala declared that Lutheran forms of worship d be used and that the Bible should have the place of pre-eminence in the service. Lutheranism was finally adopted as the state religion in 1593 when a synod at Uppsala adopted the Augsburg Confession and forbade other religions. However, the Reformation in Sweden was never as major an upheaval as in the countries on the Continent. To this day the Church of Sweden claims apostolic succession and retains a number of the medieval practices and vestments. Since the days of the Reformation, Sweden has had a "folk church," with church and state and populace yoked together in an official yet fragile relationship.

Today all Swedish citizens are automatically members of the state church if they or their parents have been baptized. Membership has literally nothing to do with one's own personal religious convictions. Since 1860 it has been possible for Swedish citizens to withdraw from the church, but until 1951 this permission was not granted unless the individual agreed to join another Christian church. Only about 1 percent of the members have bothered to leave. Today the overwhelming majority of Swedes—over 95 percent—are still officially members of the state church.

The chief function of the Church of Sweden in the eyes of the state is that of bookkeeper. The pastor's office records all births, confirmations, marriages, and deaths; and it is only on such occasions that most Swedes show their identification with the church. Though 87 percent of Swedish youth are still confirmed in the church, probably less than 5 percent of them retain any sense of loyalty after confirmation.

Several "free" churches moved into Sweden in the last century, notably the Methodist, Baptist, Missions Covenant, and the Pentecostal sects. Although these churches have greater strength proportionately because of their voluntary affiliation and more strict behavioral requirements, their influence is minimal and their membership is steadily decreasing. It has been predicted that by 1980 the free churches will have lost one-third of their present membership. The Catholic Church is a small group, gaining new members primarily through marriage and immigration.

Despite the union of church and state, the compulsory instruction in religion in the schools, and other outward evidences of religiosity, Sweden today is on the whole indifferent to the church. This benign neglect has replaced an earlier hostility caused by the resistance of the church at the beginning of this century to the needs of the common man and the subsequent social legislation. As Leslie Hunter has written: "The Lutheran Churches have in the past not been sympathetic towards or cooperative in the long struggle of 'the common man' to achieve political status, social justice and economic freedom. The social democratic movements, not unnaturally, therefore, have tended to become anti-clerical. . . ." [21]

This conflict emerged into the open in the nineteenth century, when the clergy lost their privileged status with the writing of the new constitution. The rift widened as Sweden steadily became more industrialized and urbanized. With the process of urbanization the church lost the close personal contact with her parishioners which she had formerly maintained in an intimate rural setting. The church, with her vast ownership of lands and rural mentality, was never able to comprehend this sweeping transformation of society, and she chose to resist rather than join forces of modernization. Berndt Gustafsson, the head of *Religionssociologiska Institutet* in Stockholm has written of this conflict: "The Social-Democratic party . . . came into open conflict with the Church in its very first years. It demanded disestablishment and the nationalization of all superfluous ecclesiastical property and maintained that religious instruction in the schools should be undenominational. There was sharp and unrestrained criticism of the Church in its press and public agitation. In labour disputes the clergy often sided with the employers and when such an incident occurred in 1914, the clergy openly canvassing for strike-breakers, a banner was carried at that year's First of May demonstration inscribed with the words, 'Down with priestcraft.' Even where such incidents had not taken place, the Social Democratic party in its first decades was characterized by a strong anti-clericalism." [22]

Today the Swedish people can be divided into three general groups: the farmers, small in number, who still fit into the church's pattern; the white-collar workers, who are no longer actively involved in the church; and the laborers, who, by and large, relinquished active membership earlier in the century. Most of the people and the government are no longer vigorously antichurch since the earlier battles for decent social legislation for the working man have long been forgotten. The situation today is that most people just do not even think about the church except on bookkeeping occasions and on days of sentimental value. Although the Church of Sweden claims to be suffering from a major shortage of pastors, a recent poll of laymen indicated that only one out of every hundred interviewed thought that more pastors were essential.

There is a genuine possibility that within a decade or so church and state will be officially separated. If this does not happen, there will be two primary reasons for the delay. First, there are many nontheological problems that need to be solved prior to disestablishment. Who owns the present church buildings and other holdings, the church or state? In the future who will finance the maintenance and renovation of the many beautiful cathedrals and the abundance of lovely small churches? A tiny segment of the population could never afford this. A second reason is that the government under the present arrangement exercises power over the church that she would not have with disestablishment. The government appoints the bishops, has authority over the use of a large portion of church funds, can require the church to marry divorced persons and enforce her will in other important ways.

It seems clear that the Church of Sweden would never have agreed in 1958 to ordain women had it not been for the power of the government-appointed Minister of Ecclesiastical Affairs and other government leaders to lobby so vigorously that they reversed a church resolution of a year earlier forbidding women clergy. It is surprising to note how seriously this decision to ordain women still rankles the church today, another indication of the backwardness of the church. Some conservative church leaders are so disturbed with having women clergy that they are claiming that there are now two Lutheran Churches in Sweden: the state church, which since the decision of 1958 can no longer claim to be apostolic; and the true "church within the church," which claims to remain true to the apostolic heritage by not recognizing female priests.

The greatest challenge facing the Church of Sweden today is the pragmatic orientation of an urbanized, industrialized wealth-and-welfare modern Sweden. The Churches of Sweden —and one includes in this category the "free" churches—have for the most part not been able to respond positively and creatively to the new democratic, pluralistic, and experimental life style. They have failed to understand that when they speak in the authoritarian stance of an era long gone, only the very small group of faithful followers truly "hear" what they are saying. To take one clear-cut example: in 1951, the bishops published their now famous letter which stated that all premarital sex was wrong because it conflicted with the will of God as expressed in Holy Scripture. This letter, reaffirmed in 1965, argued from an authoritarian "God-says-because-the-Bible-says" stance that quite frankly does not communicate with most Swedes today. It identified the "Christian" response with a specific code of behavior that made more sense in the sixteenth century than it does in the twentieth. Since this particular formulation is one that most Swedes cannot accept, the implication for many of them is that Christianity no longer has anything to say to them. Recently a study was made of the sexual attitudes of church members. Approximately 11 percent of the Swedish population goes to church at least once a month; this includes both the state and free churches. Seventy percent of these people believe that it is permissible for engaged couples to have sexual relations, and 50 percent gave the same approval for couples "going steady." The significance of this study is that church people who are traditionally conservative on such matters are now flouting the directive of the bishops of the Church of Sweden.

The churches have taken a similar uncompromising stand against divorce, homosexuality, and other historically deviant forms of social behavior. There has been some reinterpretation of the traditional attitude toward abortion, but this change has taken place essentially because of the demands of a secular society. Generally, the response of the church to such avant-garde writers as Eva Moberg, Lars Ullerstam, and Knut Lagrup has been negative. The church has opposed the liberalization of laws concerning sexual relations between consenting adults and censorship of films and literature. Sex education in the Swedish schools received ecclesiastical anointment only after the program had received widespread public support. Even Sweden's current concern for planned parenthood and the world population problem has until very recently received little encouragement from the churches. Little wonder, then, that Donald S. Connery, in his recent study *The Scandinavians,* refers quite appropriately to Swedish pastors as "the quiet clergy." [23] In fact, as Lars Gustafsson states: "One might say, with some degree of correctness, that the representatives of Christianity during the last decade have not played any influential part in the Swedish debate on ideas, but have preferred a position of observation with their comments limited to the specifically Christian sector of the newspapers and periodicals." [24]

This is not to say that the churches should approve of premarital sex or any other practice that they consider to be wrong. But it is to say that their teaching must be undergirded by the kind of evidence and rationale that makes sense to the pragmatic human situation of our day. The theological understanding of man and the world in which he lives and his relationship to his fellowmen has changed as radically as have his scientific and social perspectives.

There is no intended implication here that the churches of Sweden have no real concern for the moral and social issues of the present. Of course they do! The point is that their influence would be so much more pervasive and relevant if their stance could change from one of sixteenth-century authoritarianism to twentieth-century pragmatism. There is a small but significant group of priests and a larger group of laymen who are deeply sensitive to the needs of the present day and are seeking to move their churches into this modern world. But so many of these noble efforts are retarded and sometimes opposed by the heavy hand of ecclesiastical conservatism. When the former editor of *Vår Kyrka* (Our Church), the Church of Sweden's weekly newspaper, suggested a more pragmatic approach to premarital sex, a petition was signed by 630 clergymen demanding that he retract his position. Carl Gustaf Boëthius was eventually forced out of his position as editor, but the Swedish government has appreciated his prophetic role by placing him on the Royal Commission to study the program of sex education. Ingmar Ström, the lay director of the State Church's Central Board, recently wrote a confirmation book, *Kom och Se* ("Come and See"), which received widespread favorable coverage in the secular press. Ström confronted honestly and forthrightly the moral dilemmas facing young people today and suggested answers that would make sense in terms of their own personal experience. He neither condemned nor approved premarital sex, but stressed the importance of responsibility and the need to understand sexual intercourse within the context of human relationships. What he considered essential is a genuine concern for the other person as a person. Ström suggested five guidelines for making moral decisions: (1) "Give—not take," that is, seek to love rather than be loved; (2) Exploiting others for one's own selfish benefit is not love; (3) Breaking off deep personal relationships can be painful, and, therefore, the deepest physical involvement of sex must not be engaged in superficially or casually; (4) Once one has engaged in sexual intercourse with a person, there is no way to remove that experience which could on a later occasion prove to be destructive; (5) A willingness to wait for what is of deepest value often distinguishes the mature person from the casual exploiter. Ström's basic point was that sex should not be entered into lightly, but only with full consideration of the possible consequences. However, his thoughtful book was refused official sanction by the bishops on the grounds that it was not authoritarian enough in its approach to moral and social issues and not sufficiently Lutheran on matters of dogma. Most confirmation books win official acceptance by skirting the basic moral and social issues and by adopting a safe and noncontroversial theological stance.

It is too early yet to say whether the Church of Sweden will make the radical change necessary to meet the needs and demands of the present day. There is some hope that the prophetic spirit of the late Nathan Söderblom, whose one hundredth birthday was commemorated in 1966, has not been fully quenched. Just as Swedish intellectuals may be breaking out of their traditional isolationism and joining the rest of the world, respected and progressive church leaders could lead the church to speak to the frustrations and aspirations of modern man in ways which he can comprehend and to which he can respond. In a profound sense the Swedes are a deeply religious people who have lost their way in the traditional forms of creedal and liturgical expression but who grope for new insights in the search for meaning. Two recent studies by Karl-Manfred Olsson, *Kontakt med Kyrkan* and *Kristendom Demokrati Arbete,* stress this basic religious concern, which is combined with an indifference to the present structure, language, and creeds of the church. If the church can respond courageously to this new challenge of a pragmatic and pluralistic society, she may once again become a vigorous force in the life of the people whom she exists to serve. This is a lesson that the churches in the United States also need to learn.

Four

RESPONSIBLE
SEXUALITY

Anyone who is sensitive to the contemporary social scene is aware of the sheer magnitude of the problems that Americans confront in developing norms for sexual behavior. As indicated in the Introduction, the divorce rate is rising, family life is more fragile, the number of illegitimate children is steadily climbing, and venereal disease has reached epidemic proportions. The old approaches to these problems, which have been advocated by both church and state, no longer seem to work. New and fresh solutions are desperately needed.

The primary task of contemporary American society is to develop a responsible sexuality which will honor the dignity of man and also apply to the realities of the modern era. Obviously no moral code can work for all men at all times in a pluralistic society. Mankind is finite in nature, heterogeneous in background, and cosmopolitan in interests. The social goal is not to find an infallible model for responsible sexuality which would cover all situations since this would be impossible, but, rather, to provide appropriate guidelines for sexual conduct which could be adapted to fit any situation an individual might confront.

Two factors must be underscored in this search for a responsible sexuality. First, American society lives in the time of the vanishing moral absolute. The only certain conviction we know is that there is no certain conviction. We can no longer distinguish in clear-cut fashion between right and wrong, good and bad, true and false. The more we know, the more we realize what we do not know. The information explosion has increased intellectual and moral skepticism. Moral decisions have always been ambiguous since they involve a weighing of alternatives and consequences. A man is moral only if he is free to make decisions on the basis of incomplete evidence. Yet in the not too distant past, certainly in the nineteenth century, our society had a rather clear notion as to what forms of sexual behavior and social relationships were to be preferred. Chastity before marriage, especially for women, was expected, and divorce was either prohibited or strongly discouraged. Artificial birth control was in many places illegal and abortions were prohibited. The single person was expected to refrain from sexual relationships. Masturbation was considered a sin or a disease and homosexuality a crime. To be sure, individuals often did not live up to these ideals, but usually at the risk of guilt or social disapproval.

In our day such traditional sexual norms are widely questioned. Other considerations are deemed equally important in shaping sexual behavior: length of engagement, fragility of a marriage, availability of contraceptives, and social background. Such ambiguity increases the difficulty of making moral decisions, but this is a frank acknowledgment of the kind of world in which we live. Our society has undergone a profound transformation in what it tolerates as permissible behavior, and even more important, there now exists public acknowledgment of great uncertainty about what is permissible. The communications media are filled with frank discussions of "The Sex Revolution," a factor that was not true ten years ago. Former Secretary of State Dean Rusk's confession to a group of young people about the complexities of the world political situation could be applied just as well to the sexual realm: "If you think you're confused, take heart. You're only in touch with reality."

Secondly, we note in society the gradual disappearance of the double standard for male and female. If men can vote, so can women. If men can be educated and become doctors, writers, lawyers, and teachers, women can too. And if men desire sexual freedom, why shouldn't women? In the past, society and the church have exhibited an overwhelming bias against women which stamped them as inferior beings. Their place in society was strictly limited to specific tasks and occupations. Their sexual role was to remain passive recipients who submitted to male aggressiveness and superiority. However, in our day such treatment is being denounced as male chauvinism. The feminist movement, showing strength and vigor unknown since the early part of the century, seeks not only to change the laws that still discriminate against women, but even more crucial, to destroy the traditional notion of man as the breadwinner and head of the house, and the woman as the subordinate companion. This movement seeks equal opportunity for men and women—in raising children, supervising household duties and engaging in occupations outside the home. What counts is the humanity of the individual, not a fixed rule surrounding his or her sex. This is exactly the point Henrik Ibsen made in *A Doll's House*:

HELMER: It's shocking. This is how you would neglect your most sacred duties.

NORA: What do you consider my most sacred duties?

HELMER: Do I need to tell you that? Are they not your duties to your husband and your children?

NORA: I have other duties just as sacred.
HELMER: That you have not. What duties could those be?
NORA: Duties to myself.
HELMER: But before all else you are a wife and mother.
NORA: I don't believe that any longer. I believe that above all
          else I am a reasonable human being just as you are—
          or, at all events, that I must try to become one.[1]

Heretofore male and female have been understood almost
exclusively in terms of their biological make-up, and this physiological difference has been used to justify traditional roles.
Today, however, we know that there is no such creature as
the pure male or female. Each person in varying degree has
secondary characteristics of the other sex. Male and female
are usually distinguished genetically, with the male having
XY sex chromosomes and the female XX sex chromosomes.
Our increased knowledge has indicated that what is of crucial
importance is the "psychophysical" sexual characteristics,
which are a product of environmental factors. From this perspective sexual behavior is an acquired characteristic determined in large part by the expectations of a particular society.
Although societies differ with respect to their social preferences, each one does tend to develop a conception of what
constitutes proper male and female behavior. This norm becomes so pervasive that it is then considered to be hereditary
rather than environmental. In our society, as soon as a child is
born, a mass of social expectations surrounds that child, one
type if the child is a boy and another if it is a girl. A male baby
is treated differently than a girl baby, and this gives rise to
qualities and attitudes which are wrongly suspected of having
a genetic basis. A well-known nursery rhyme illustrates how
different are the social expectations for boys and girls:

> What are little boys made of, made of?
> What are little boys made of?
> Frogs and snails, and puppy-dogs' tails;
> And that's what little boys are made of.

What are little girls made of, made of?
What are little girls made of?
Sugar and spice, and all that's nice;
And that's what little girls are made of.

The shape of one's sexuality is determined in large part by the expectations of his society. Once we learn this elemental fact, we will no longer place male and female in rigidly separate categories. Each individual will be understood in the context of his own particular heredity and environment. We will try to create a society which will, above all, respect the humanity of the individual and not his traditional sex role.

Despite the gradual disappearance of the double standard, there is as much sexual segregation in work outside the home today as there was sixty years ago. Although over one-third of all women are now employed, the vast majority are confined to occupations that our society has traditionally classified as female. The United States is wasting valuable resources by discriminating against women for employment as doctors, lawyers, teachers, social workers, and other essential occupations at the same time that severe shortages exist in these areas.

Responsible sexuality will remain a pipe dream until mankind takes seriously the conviction that men and women are to be treated as equals. Only then will society understand the radical changes that must take place in the structure of marriage and the family. The objective is not to destroy monogamous marriage and the family, but rather, to destroy the conditions within these institutions which have placed woman in an inferior role. This is an absolute prerequisite for responsible sexuality.

Keeping in mind, then, the temper of the times and the equal worth of each individual, male and female, what is a workable social model for responsible sexuality? We can clarify matters by distinguishing between authoritarian morality and hedonistic morality. Authoritarian morality looks to the past for rules or prohibitions to determine proper sexual behavior. We have already referred to the position of the Church of Sweden concerning premarital sex. This position, made explicit in the Bishops' Letter of 1951 and reaffirmed in 1965, states that premarital sex is contrary to the will of God as expressed in Holy Scripture. The typical approach of this morality is to place the norm for sexual morality in the Bible or the church, the former for traditional Protestants and the latter for traditional Catholics.

The weaknesses to this approach for today seem obvious. First, authoritarian morality, in establishing a basis for all sexual behavior, attempts to establish a moral absolute. Such an absolute is no longer possible. For example, the Roman Catholic Church still officially teaches that artificial birth control is contrary to God's will. Such a teaching is not realistic in a world inundated by a population explosion that threatens its very existence. This church further insists that the sole purpose of sex is for procreation, which severely curtails the positive function that sex can have in enhancing a human relationship. Many Catholics today refuse to follow the teachings of their church on these matters. Although the Pope has recently issued an encyclical prohibiting the use of artificial birth control, many priests and laymen openly flout his teaching. They see his mandate as psychologically damaging to the individual and causing an unnecessary rift within the church. Secondly, the position of Bible or church on sexual matters is not always explicit and often varies according to the circumstances. Indeed the Bible is a bundle of contradictions and inconsistencies regarding sex, reflecting changing times and conditions. For example, the Old Testament approves of polygyny under certain conditions, and the Apostle Paul clearly preferred celibacy over matrimony. The churches of today would most likely regard both of these teachings as outmoded, and if this be the case with respect to polygyny and celibacy, what about premarital sex and divorce? The plain fact of the matter is that Scripture does not consistently teach any specific laws of sexual behavior. Thirdly, most church members today frankly do not regard the Bible or the church as the final arbiter for making decisions about matters of sex. Truth in morality is determined by man's own judgment to decide what makes sense to him rather than depending on an outside authority such as church or Bible. The late Pope John contributed to this shift of authority in the determination of truth when he stated in his final encyclical that each individual should worship God according to the dictates of his own conscience. If this is applicable in the paramount matter of man's worship of God, it is surely applicable in his approach to sexual matters. The traditional Roman Catholic submission to the authority of the church and the Protestant reliance on the testimony of Scripture are being rapidly replaced by the tests of reason and experience. The basic conviction of modern man is that he can no longer accept the "thou shalt nots" of authoritarian morality without first examining their validity in terms of his own experience. The Bible and the church can only suggest general guidelines for proper behavior and indeed they should. But in the final analysis the commandments of the past cannot determine what should be the imperatives of the present.

Hedonistic morality puts the emphasis on personal pleasure and the present as the arbiter for sexual behavior. The Sixth Commandment of the late Swedish writer Lars Gyllensten characterizes this position: "Thou shalt not spread venereal diseases, or bring unwanted children into the world, or expose other people to sexual violence . . . for the rest, you may devote yourself freely to [whatever] . . . your animal nature . . . may cause you to desire." [2] According to Gyllensten and his followers, man is basically an animal who has sexual urges that need to be fulfilled. He ought to be permitted to fulfill these needs as long as he does not harm another person.

The weakness to this hedonistic morality is twofold. First, it degrades man by describing him as just another animal; it considers his biological urge and the pursuit of pleasure the epitome of sexuality. The most popular exhibit at the Stockholm Museum of Modern Art a few years ago was an eighty-two foot long, thirty-foot wide, six ton pop-art replica of a woman lying on her back. Through this maze of wire, fabric, and glue—called by the universal term "she"—it was possible to walk and find symbolism relevant to each portion of the female torso. "She" and her body were one and the same. This morality cheapens sexuality by turning it into exclusively physical gratification. It is little wonder that some proponents of hedonistic morality in Sweden are now publicly advocating the "thrill" of extramarital affairs and a preference for short-term marriages. The ideal would be to take a husband or wife for a few years and then swap around for the rest of one's virile life, letting the state take care of the children. These same individuals are urging the return of legalized houses of prostitution for both men and women on the principle of the right of the individual to gratify his animal nature. These suggestions are entirely consistent with the maxim of hedonistic morality, that is, "that you may devote yourself freely to [whatever] your animal nature desires."

A second weakness to this view is that it leads to the breakdown of covenants of stability and trust between man and woman, relationships which are important to marriage and the family. If sex is but a biological urge, then it does not really matter how or with whom that urge is fulfilled. There is no place for a special dimension of loving concern which gives character to the sex act. There is no need for tenderness and compassion. Such a view is repugnant to those of us who continue to defend marriage and the family as an important and stabilizing force in our chaotic world and who further believe that sex without compassion is like a body without a soul. These structures of marriage and the family are not perfect, but they are better than anything else we have at present.

Both hedonistic and authoritarian morality tend to stress the sex act itself as the sole basis for moral judgment. The former suggests that the sex act can be performed under any conditions as long as no one is hurt. The latter insists that performing the sex act outside of the marriage relationship is wrong. In neither case is the character of the individual or the relationship between the participants considered paramount. This basic weakness is common to both forms of morality.

SEXUAL BEHAVIOR IN SOCIETY

Responsible sexuality puts the emphasis on the quality of the human relationship and not on the sex act itself. It insists that what is worth preserving in the older patterns of sexual behavior must be defended on pragmatic rather than authoritarian grounds. It does not simply cast aside all teachings of authoritarian morality, but preserves those teachings which are consistent with the best in human encounters. Responsible sexuality agrees with hedonistic morality in taking into account the reality of the present situation and the satisfaction of sexual urges, but responsible sexuality also insists that these considerations must be placed in the larger context of past teachings and future consequences. Man does not live only in and for the present. Responsible sexuality affirms three principles.

First, the focus for proper sexual behavior is love. There is no word in any language more difficult to define than "love." It can mean lust (self-aggrandizement), philia (friendship), eros (the drive to create) and agape (primary concern for the other). Our meaning of love includes all these concepts but puts them in the framework of agape. "Love" is primarily a verb and not a noun. It is a process of

total involvement with another individual, with his uniqueness as well as his common humanity. Man fulfills himself in
his meeting with the other. As the Jewish theologian Martin
Buber puts it: "All real living is meeting." Love is not a
single emotion, but a totality of encounter with another person. Sex is not an isolated phenomenon which can be dis-
sected as a separate function or entity. Sex has meaning only
in the context of human relationships. It has implications for
both the personal and social dimensions of the individual, for
his marriage and his family. Although this may seem obvious,
it is a point too often neglected. Too many books on sex deal
with the specifics of intercourse and not with the wholeness
of human life.

Responsible sexuality recognizes, to use Martin Buber's
terms, that each person is a Thou rather than an It. For
Buber man's relationship to the world and to other people is
twofold: I-Thou and I-It. Each of these relationships involves
a different kind of knowledge and in each our response is
different. In the I-It relationship, we look upon the other
person as a thing—an It—to be manipulated for our own
ends. The other person becomes an object which we con-
sume for our own selfish interests. In the I-Thou relationship
the other person is a person like ourselves, with his own
interests and integrity. We cannot manipulate the other for
our own sake, for the moment that we do, the Thou becomes
an It.

Buber maintains that the history of the individual and of
the human race both indicate a progressive augmentation of
the world of It. Our age is becoming more and more me-
chanical and impersonal, and the real crisis of our time is
the need to rediscover the personal dimension—the reality
and depth of genuine interpersonal confrontations. We could
illustrate the augmentation of the world of I-It from many
different areas: the movies, literature, and popular music. We
could also illustrate it with the popular notion of marriage

and love as lust emanating from Hollywood—what J. B. Priestly has called eroticism. He notes that eroticism ". . . is sexual pleasure without sexual responsibility . . . it is the furthest possible removed from love, which is supremely personal. . . . Nothing worth calling a relationship can be created by it. . . . The other sex is not really there in its true complementary character." [3]

Responsible sexuality maintains that sex can best be appreciated and fulfilled within the context of a love relationship. There is no such thing as the victor and the vanquished in this kind of partnership. The one person cannot "con" the other person into sex and thereby treat her as an object of his own desire. Both parties must be willing to engage honestly and freely in this culminating act of love, for this is the deepest expression and fulfillment of a personal encounter. Love includes tenderness, compassion, fidelity, and trust. To be sure, the principle of love is not a blueprint which can make explicit what one's proper action should be in every situation. But it is a basic frame of reference that will give integrity to one's decisions.

Second, responsible sexuality stresses the importance of time and consequences. One does not normally "fall in love" overnight or even over a period of a few weeks. Love requires time to deepen and enrich, and to be properly appreciated, the sex act should come as the fulfillment of this deepening experience in the same way that the marriage vow is the culmination of a period of courtship and growing together. There are men who operate on the assumption that a few dates with a girl is an automatic wholesale invitation to intercourse. This is a degrading abuse of a friendship and is virtually a guarantee for future infidelity. The factor of time is of immense importance in the maturation process. "Love is patient and kind; love is not jealous or boastful; it is not arrogant or rude" (I Corinthians 13:4–5).

Of equal importance is the wider perspective in terms of

consequences. Herein lies the weakness of so-called situation ethics, which permits conduct to be determined primarily by the particular situation. To be sure, love is a principle which is dependent in part for its implementation on the particular situation. But the problem is which situation? James Gustafson, Professor of Christian Ethics at Yale Divinity School, makes a very telling criticism of Joseph Fletcher's situation ethics: "If the situation is to determine what love requires, it is terribly important how one understands his situation. Is it boy plus girl between 1:00 a.m. and 3:00 a.m. after a number of drinks in a motel room who feel affection for each other . . . or is it boy, responsible to others than the girl, and responsible to and for her over a long period of time under a covenant of some sort, plus girl concerned not only for the present moment but for the past and future relationships as well, in a human community for whose vitality and order they have responsibility and which in turn has to seek its common good?" [4]

A proper regard for the situation includes an awareness of future consequences. An affirmation of love involves a concern not only for present biological desires on the part of two persons, but also a responsibility to parents and other loved ones as well as plans and dreams for the future. The wider perspective in terms of time and consequences is all important.

Third, there is the importance of fidelity, stability, and trust. This is the real value of the institution of marriage and the marriage vow—that there is a covenant which exists between a man and a woman who promise to love and cherish each other in a partnership of permanence: "I, John, take Thee, Mary, to be my wedded wife. And I do promise and covenant before God and these witnesses to be thy loving and faithful husband. In plenty and in want; in joy and in sorrow; in sickness and in health; as long as we both shall live."

This is probably the most important promise that two persons will ever make together. The promise is of primary importance, and the sex act is one significant dimension of this deeper covenant. Marriage is not just jumping in and out of bed. Marriage is trust and tenderness—and jumping into bed —and kids and colds and earaches and finances—and jumping into bed—and laughter and tears and hope and despair— and jumping into bed. The chances are that a permanent relationship, with both its sickness and its health, is the strongest guarantee for a wholesome sex life. It is the best that we have to show that ". . . love bears all things, believes all things, hopes all things, endures all things" (I Corinthians 13:7).

Sex, then, should be judged in terms of relationships and not of genital acts. In this sense promiscuity takes on a different meaning. Whereas heretofore promiscuity was defined in terms of the sex act outside of marriage, now it should be defined in terms of the quality of the encounter both within and without marriage. Promiscuity involves taking advantage of another person. With the gradual emancipation of women today, there is far less promiscuity than in the past, when women often had to use their bodies as a means of gaining acceptance. Women today demand integrity and respect in their new role. The Swedes have often been accused of being promiscuous people, but it could be that Americans are far more promiscuous. Lester Kirkendall suggests: "If we were to talk about promiscuity—casual and exploitive intercourse —then I would be willing to wager there is more in the United States than in Sweden. Probably fewer Swedish girls go into marriage as virgins, however, than is the case with American youth, because once a responsible, affectional basis for a relationship is recognized, intercourse is less severely frowned upon in Sweden than in the United States." [5] The Swedes do not consider promiscuity in terms of the sex act per se but in terms of the *total* involvement—whether there is or is not a mutuality of tenderness and honesty between the two partners. If there is, then the use of sex is not promiscuous. If there is not, then sex becomes promiscuous whether or not the partners are married. This seems to be a much more sensible view of promiscuity than the genital one.

Premarital Sex: A special situation arises with respect to premarital sex. Unmarried lovers are more free to experiment, to try new life styles without the financial burdens and other obligations of a permanent commitment. The ready availability of effective contraceptives eliminates the fear of an unwanted pregnancy. Two types of individuals should be distinguished in matters related to premarital sex. The first type of couple is the man and woman who are engaged or who have committed themselves to probable marriage or who are living together in a marriage-type relationship. In this case, a strong sense of commitment to one another exists, and a genuine responsibility for the possible consequences of a coital relationship. The other type of couple is one having a "meaningful friendship," but who have made no definite commitment to each other for the future. The rationale for or against sexual intercourse in this case is far less clear. A so-called meaningful friendship can mean most anything that the couple, or one of them, want it to mean; there is less likelihood that fidelity and a concern for consequences will be taken into account. What guidelines can we suggest?

Premarital sexual behavior, like all forms of sexual behavior, must be judged in the context of human relationships and not specific acts. Lester Kirkendall makes this point nicely in his book *Premarital Intercourse and Interpersonal Relationships*: "The moral code of society today is primarily focused on acts. So long as we focus on the absence or occurrence of specific acts as our basis for making moral decisions and judgments, we will be defeated in trying to think constructively about motivation, meaning, and the consequences of behavior for interpersonal relationships. In premarital sexual behavior we ordinarily consider participation in a sexual act as an evidence of immorality. If we accept the improvement of interpersonal relations as a criterion for moral judgments, then we find that some very immoral experiences may occur in the realm of sex without any overt sexual action having occurred." [6]

The question for premarital sexual behavior today is not whether one should remain a virgin until marriage, for this is to put the entire emphasis on the sex act itself. Thus the equation of virginity with virtue should no longer be the decisive factor in our evaluation. The question today is whether the commitment of two individuals is so based on love, tenderness, and fidelity that the sex act truly deepens this relationship; or whether the sex act based exclusively on biological gratification is not in fact a perversion of an individual or of the couple. If it is the former, that is, an honest and mutual fulfillment, then the two partners must decide whether they are prepared to bear the consequences of such an act now— including possible feelings of guilt—or wait until their love has matured in depth and intensity. Since promiscuity can occur within as well as without marriage, why should we condone it in the first instance and condemn it in the latter? The same reasoning can be applied to petting and mutual masturbation. Whether such activity is promiscuous depends on the commitment and not on whether one always stops short of ejaculation or orgasm. The Swedes are right in that the standard for judging the validity of both petting and intercourse should be: with whom and for what purpose? There is nothing good or bad in such activities in themselves.

In the case of the couple who have pledged themselves to marry, it seems clear that intercourse can be quite acceptable. Our society has been unrealistic in teaching that the wedding night should mark a radical change in the physical relationship between two loved ones. This sudden "turning it on" can often cause unnecessary tensions that only compound the difficulties of adjustment to married life. It would seem more sensible that once the pledge to marry has been made in good faith, a man and a woman, as they share dreams for the future, can often experience in sexual intimacy a genuine and intense acknowledgment of their love. Here sexual experimentation has an important role to fulfill, provided that both partners agree that consummation is desirable. A gradual sexual adjustment over a period of many months can make the first stages of married life much more harmonious. Whatever decision is made should be arrived at mutually, lovingly, and with full responsibility for possible consequences.

It is impossible to generalize as to whether engaged couples who have sexual relations are then able to make a better sexual adjustment in marriage. Morton Hunt argues: "Any number of moralists have warned the young that premarital intercourse cheapens or harms their later relationship, but the objective evidence does not sustain them: the most reliable interviews and surveys available show, for instance, that the great majority of women who slept with their fiancés before marriage feel that it strengthened the relationship; that only a very small minority have guilt feelings or regret about it after marriage; and that women who had successful premarital intercourse far more often achieve sexual adjustment in marriage than do those who stayed virginal." [7]

Credit for satisfactory sexual adjustment, however, may be due more to the temperament of the couple than the fact that they had engaged in premarital sex. This is Alfred Kinsey's surmise: "The most responsive females may have been the ones who had had the largest amount of premarital experience and because they were responsive, they were the ones who had most often reached orgasm in marriage. The females who had abstained before marriage may have been the physiologically less responsive individuals who, therefore, were the ones who had most often remained chaste, both before and after marriage." [8]

It is important that engaged couples not rush into marriage

for the sake of sex or for any other reason. Half of the women in the United States marry before age twenty. These women have about three times as high a chance of divorce as women who marry in their twenties. It would be better in most cases for couples to delay marriage until they are adequately prepared for this important compact even if this means that they would engage in premarital sex. We would do well to imitate the Swedish way for engaged couples.

When we consider the action of a couple who justify a sexual relationship on the grounds of "meaningful friendship," the case for intercourse is much more ambiguous. The growth of a large adolescent subculture with excessive freedom and limited responsibilities has literally thrown young people into situations of relationship and intimacy. Also, the anonymity of the larger urban areas has loosened the ties of family stability and made possible many types of liaisons. Most of these friendships can be rationalized as "special" at one time or another. But can intercourse be justified on the grounds, or on the hope, of developing a meaningful friendship? Probably not, because of the lack of any mutual commitment in addition to the danger of sex becoming something casual and as ordinary as an evening meal. It loses, in fact, its essential quality as an I-Thou relationship. This is precisely the difficulty with Swedish permissiveness. Although the Swedes affirm that sex should be a dimension of a deeper involvement, one doubts that this is possible when sex becomes so commonplace. Much of the exhibitionism of recent literature, drama, and movies describes or depicts in minute detail all the variations of the sex act. Sex becomes an object of public scrutiny and loses its intimacy and mystery. In this day of increasing impersonalism, public exhibitionism, and permissiveness, it is important that we insist on the wonder surrounding the sex act as perhaps the last bastion for privacy. It is ironic that in this day of easy mobility, when privacy is so easily obtained, sex actually becomes more public and less intimate. Just as a woman is most attractive and inviting, not when she is completely naked, but when covered by at least a fig leaf, so too is sex more exhilarating and beautiful when it remains something hidden and private. The sex act should help one to express his personality in all intensity and fullness and joy; this can best be achieved within the shared and private world of two persons who are deeply in love. Sex based on friendship can so easily degenerate to casual gratification without ever rising to love.

The new puritanism of permissiveness can be as abusive of the self as the old puritanism of abstinence. Whereas the old doctrine declared: "Thou shalt not have sexual relations before marriage," the new puritanism affirms: "Thou shalt have sexual relations before marriage." If the old puritanism made a person feel guilty if he did have premarital sexual relations, the new puritanism makes him feel guilty if he does not. In either case there is undue social pressure. Sex obsession is as neurotic as sex repression. Unbridled freedom and stern repression both produce anxiety and conflict as both types of puritanism put the stress on the sex act itself and thereby deny the importance of the total relationship. It is crucial that sex be united with love in the same way that freedom is yoked with responsibility.

Sexual pleasure outside of a love encounter is indeed real, but in most cases it would be wise for those couples who are having a meaningful friendship to play it cool and conservative. The odds are that the waiting game will be the best guarantee for future happiness. If a couple still wishes to have intercourse on the basis of a good friendship, they should be willing to ask themselves: Why are we becoming so intimately involved? Is there mutual trust and concern? Are we really seeking for the deep union of two persons or are we seeking for our own physical gratification? Are we prepared for all the consequences? Just as a woman often does not know that she is pregnant until a certain length of time after conception, so too do a man or woman not realize the emotional scars that may appear much later—feelings of guilt that cannot be easily erased, perhaps disappointment in the sex act itself, which can bring forth feelings of inadequacy and inferiority. These are real possibilities that cannot be ignored.

Some individuals argue that one should engage in frequent sexual experimentation before marriage in order to learn the tricks of the trade. The shallowness of this reasoning lies not only in its making sex seem casual but in that it seems to guarantee sexual salvation through technique. How many partners should one have before he is considered knowledge-able and ready to advance to marriage? Surely a more likely way of guaranteeing marital stability is to confine such experimentation to one's future marriage partner. This would be a confirmation of the importance a human being attaches to dignity and self-respect for the other person.

Responsible premarital sexuality does not permit easy answers. It would be simpler to say, as the old morality does, that one should act a certain way in all situations. But to be human is to be uncertain. To be human is to make judgments based on limited information, knowing that one may well be wrong. Man is not a computer into which all the data and potential situations can be programed. In the ambiguity of moral dilemmas man must do the best he can. This is why it is so crucial that future consequences and the importance of fidelity and trust be taken into consideration before a decision is made. Only in this larger context can wise judgments be forthcoming.

Marriage and the Family: In most cases, pragmatically speaking, it is wise to confine the sexual act within the marriage promise since, as we have noted, it is this covenant which seeks to guarantee fidelity and to take the longer perspective. Monogamous marriage is not part-and-parcel of the natural and divine order, nor has it been the only type of marriage in every society. Monogamous marriage can be best defended as a time-tested, worthwhile haven, based on shared trust and fidelity in a world which, because of its crass impersonalism and frightful insecurity, makes this covenant so essential to human stability and sanity. Sex should be a grand and glorious dimension of married life. It is not to be considered dirty nor degrading. A woman should derive as much fulfillment from it as a man. The old Victorians were as wrong in their debasement of sex as the new Victorians are in their cheapening of sex. It is ironic that both the old and new Victorians have tried to separate sex and love, the former equating sex with illicit affairs outside of marriage, and thereby vulgarizing it, and the latter profaning it as the natural outcome of any "meaningful friendship." Sex and love should not be separated. It is the relationship of love that enhances sex, and not sex that creates the relationship. Yes, sex is fun! Yes, the sex act is a grandiose physical feeling. But if this is its total dimension, then we might as well develop a special computer as a kind of electronic-age prostitute to satisfy our biological urges. A marital relationship based on *tenderness*—"I love you"—*trust*—"I, John, take thee, Mary"—and *permanence* —"in plenty and in want, in joy and in sorrow, in sickness and in health"—is the best guarantee of a wholesome sex life.

Although monogamous marriage is the most acceptable pattern of sexual relationship in contemporary Western society, other forms of marriage may also work in our situation today. In particular, there should be no stigma attached to one parent families as there is nothing morally wrong for a single person to raise a child. Nor are group living arrangements to be condemned outright. The widest possible limits of permissible living arrangements should be tolerated by society. Yet, since early times, human beings have felt the need to belong to small groups, to feel wanted and loved. The larger that group has become, the more difficult it usually has been to maintain close intimate contacts. For most people a man and a woman and their small children who live together in an atmosphere of love and fidelity has proved to be the best guarantee for happiness, acceptance, and stability. Although we are being constantly reminded of the breakdown of marriage and the family in contemporary society, we need to remember that monogamous marriage and the nuclear family still have many more successes than failures, but they do not work for everyone, and in today's isolated, fragmented, highly mobile society, other living patterns—for example, group marriages and kibbutz-style arrangements—provide alternatives.

There are many ways in which current family institutions should be improved. It is imperative that the United States enact social legislation that would free the wife and mother to work outside the home. Once again we should follow the lead of Sweden in allowing for paid maternity leaves, day-care centers, child stipends, and housing allowances. The primary purpose of such legislation will be to give women and children as much dignity as men now have. Unfortunately, however, our society's negative image of the working mother is nearly as strong as our sexual taboos. The working mother who has young children is almost by definition considered neurotic. However, Betty Friedan and others have rightly pointed out that bored stay-at-home mothers are probably much more likely to become neurotic than mothers who work outside the home for their own personal fulfillment. Men and women should have equal opportunity to enrich their humanity by working outside the home and sharing the household and family responsibilities if that is their wish. The family should remain as society's best way for protecting and nurturing the young since children need to be raised by persons who really care for them. Although the kibbutz-style of raising children collectively may work in some cases, even here substitute mothers are provided, and the parents are encouraged to be with their children during certain periods of the day. Certain functions of the family, namely, proper care and love, remain crucial despite the new demands of our technological society. The stability of an individual is still dependent in large part on the stability of his family.

Divorce and Extramarital Sex: Our society has been slow to realize that in some cases—in fact, in an increasing number—marriage has become a serious detriment to the couple and their small children. The love that was originally the reason for marriage no longer exists. People do change over the years and can grow apart from one another. They can become virtual strangers and lose the common bonds of fidelity and affection that once drew them together. This is a fact of life that we should honestly acknowledge. There is nothing inherently right about holding together in marriage two people who no longer love one another. Such a marriage can be damaging both to the couple and to their children. The question ought always to be—what is the best for all concerned? And in many cases the answer should be that divorce is the best of all possible solutions. Morton Hunt writes: "The wide use of divorce today is not a sign of a diminished desire to be married, but of an increased desire to be happily married. . . . More than ever, Americans want to marry well . . . more than ever they are coming to believe that divorce is morally justifiable in terms of the well-being of all concerned. For in the light of its consequences, divorce clearly appears to be a highly moral act, not only in many specific situations but in a broader sense. It is the necessary corollary of our elevated ideal of marriage, our valuation of emotional health, and our respect for the individual's right to seek happiness." [9]

Our divorce laws should be greatly relaxed to make it possible for couples to break the legal relationship when they believe that continuing the marriage is detrimental to the individuals concerned. Fortunately our society no longer harbors a serious stigma against divorce. We are also recognizing that divorce is sometimes better for the small children involved than keeping the marriage intact for the children only to be exposed to serious marital tension. A six-month period before granting a divorce seems a reasonable length of time. Also, husband and wife should be willing to meet with a marriage counsellor or other professionally trained person to attempt to learn if their relationship can be healed, and if a longer period of waiting should be encouraged. The grounds for divorce, for example, adultery or incompatibility, are not important. Nor is it essential for the courts to decide which partner is the guilty party. It takes two to make a relationship, and both must share blame for the failure of the marriage. The essential concern is for fully adequate protection to be provided for the children. The question of child custody and alimony payments should be decided by the courts if the couple is unable to reach an amicable settlement. California, where nearly one out of every two marriages is legally terminated, has recently passed a new divorce law which could serve as a model for the other states. The only two grounds for divorce are incurable insanity and irreconcilable differences. It is no longer necessary that one of the pair be found guilty of breaking up the marriage. The waiting period for a final decree is six months, and alimony is awarded primarily on the basis of need.

However, there may be, for some couples, another alternative to divorce. This is the matter of extramarital relationships. We can state unequivocally that for most couples extramarital affairs are probably a dangerous alternative, primarily because most people have been reared to have guilt feelings about such "illicit" encounters. Moreover, fidelity is such an important value to a successful marriage that anything that subverts fidelity should be discouraged. Our study of Swedish society has indicated that although extensive permissive premarital contacts are acknowledged in Sweden, most Swedish married couples consider fidelity essential to the marriage covenant.

We must give consideration, however, to some couples who can either save their marriage or strengthen an already existing happy marriage through extramarital experiences. Are such extramarital relationships morally wrong? Once again we should answer that question in terms of the total context and not in terms of the sex act itself. If extramarital sex harms the already existing human relationships, then it is morally wrong. If extramarital sex enhances the human dimension, then it may be morally proper. As Erik Erikson has suggested: "Fidelity without a sense of diversity can become an obsession and a bore; diversity without a sense of fidelity, an empty relativism." [10] We are not suggesting here an empty relativism which has no sense of fidelity and perspective; this is morally wrong. But we are suggesting that a sense of diversity is not always improper. The whole point of responsible sexology is to put primary consideration on the relationship and not the sex act in itself. From this perspective it may be morally improper for a wife to have a cup of coffee with another man if this interferes with her attitude toward her husband and children, but it may be morally proper for her to have intercourse with another man if this helps her attitude toward her husband and children.

Let us take a hypothetical example. Suppose that there is a married woman and a married man, not her husband, who have come to know each other well over a period of time. They are both in love with their respective spouses, but they also enjoy each other's company. They find that the occasional times that they spend together are good therapy for both of them and in fact make them better persons in their commitments to others. We all know of such harmless friendships, and we see nothing morally wrong with them. Yet suppose this man and woman reach the point where they wish to have intercourse. If this does not affect their love for their families, but continues to enhance it, does genital contact make the friendship morally wrong? Our answer would be No as long as the other commitments remained the same or were improved. Or, take the situation of a man about to be divorced from his wife who makes the acquaintance of another woman. They meet and talk frequently, and she is able to make him understand that for the time being, perhaps in this particular case for the sake of the children, it would be better for him to remain married. This man and woman have intercourse, and in this encounter he is able to find compassion that in fact helps his relationship with his family. In this case an extramarital affair is a help rather than a hindrance. Alfred Kinsey and his associates question the assumption that extramarital relationships will always do damage to a marriage. They point to evidence that in some cases sexual adjustments with the spouse had improved as a result of the female's extramarital experience.[11] Gerhard Neubeck, in his book *Extramarital Relations,* writes: ". . . as long as there is marriage as a monogamous system, there will be a concomitant system of clandestine relationships, sometimes rivaling and competing with, sometimes nestling next to, the basic marriage." [12]

However, we should reiterate that in our society, which identifies sexuality with genital action, it is wise for most couples to refrain from extramarital sex. All that we suggest is that in some situations an extramarital arrangement may be the best answer to other far more unpleasant possibilities.[13] No hard and fast rule can be established, for the particular situation is important. Morton Hunt has suggested a sensible rationale for a contemporary attitude toward extramarital sex: "The emerging ethic concerning adultery is a pragmatic one, relying not upon commands from on high nor the dictates of a stern conscience, but on a prudent appraisal of the situation and the potential consequences of an action. . . . Adultery by American women is, or soon will be, on a plateau; some will do it and some won't, but by and large it will continue to be rare, unstable, and more of a threat to happiness than common sense can usually justify. . . . [This] may not be a sublime ethic, but it is at least a workable one." [14]

Other Patterns of Sexual Behavior: Another problem relates to the single person who has no present intentions of marrying or remarrying. Surely our previous standards have been cruel to these people. As long as sex was to be confined to the marriage covenant, single persons were completely beyond the pale of normal sexual activity. We now realize that single persons have their own sexual needs and interests which must be legitimated and fulfilled. Once again the important criterion is the quality of the relationship, but in the case of many single individuals even this criterion needs to be considerably modified. Consider single persons who have no intention of establishing a permanent covenant with a person of the opposite sex. They have deliberately chosen to remain single. In such cases it would seem quite proper for them to use the sexual act in a way that enhances their own well being as long as it does not injure another person. For them, temporary liaisons may prove helpful in providing them with sexual outlets while at the same time shielding them from more permanent commitments which they, for their own reasons, would prefer not to make. At the same time these individuals should also recognize that temporary liaisons might be an escape tactic from what they really need but fear, namely, an intimate and lasting relationship with another person of the opposite sex. Society should not condemn single persons for sexual contacts which do no harm but may prove enriching to the parties concerned. As we have noted, there should be greater public tolerance for single men and women who choose to raise children without marrying. State laws need to be modified to make it more possible for single persons to adopt children. Unwed mothers need to be encouraged to find that place in society which will help rather than hinder their lives and the lives of their children.

Our society must also become more tolerant of such a simple act as masturbation, the practice of sexual self-stimulation. It is a form of enjoyment that man and woman can have at any age and is a common occurrence. It seems incredible that so many witch tales have been invented to make this practice appear destructive. Masturbation has no harmful effects. It is a way of relieving frustration and is to be preferred to other sexual outlets which could do damage to another human being. Masturbation becomes a problem only when, like eating and sleeping, it becomes an obsession.

Another sexual practice is homosexuality, the sexual attachment between members of the same sex. According to Dr. Isadore Rubin: ". . . between their adolescence and old age, about thirty-seven percent of all males have some overt homosexual experience to the point of orgasm; that over half of the males who remain unmarried at thirty-five have homosexual experience; and that about four percent of all white males are exclusively homosexual all of their lives. For females, the estimated incidence of homosexual behavior is about half that for males." [15]

The traditional view of this age-old phenomenon is of a disease from which man needs to be both saved and cured. In some cases this may be true. Such individuals should receive proper medical treatment to enable them to function as heterosexual persons, and yet we should remember that there are many more sick heterosexuals than homosexuals. For some individuals, hereditary and environmental factors have combined in such a fashion to cause some males to prefer intimate male companionship, and some females to enjoy only female contacts. And yet, it must be acknowledged that each individual possesses, to some degree, both male and female traits, and that it is our psycho-physical development that determines the dominance of one trait over the other. But because there are so many unknown factors involved in this development, it is grossly unfair of society to condemn a minority of individuals for acting in a way that is most consistent with their psycho-physical make-up. Homosexuality should be neither encouraged nor condemned. It should become accepted as a legitimate form of behavior. The laws regulating homosexuality should be the same laws that regulate heterosexuality: protection of the innocent and protection against abuse. To do more than this is to attempt to legislate one form of sexual morality as normative for everyone. Homosexuals can perform as effectively and positively in society as heterosexuals.

In a free and pluralistic society the widest possible limits of adult sexual behavior should be tolerated. Whatever consenting adults wish to do in private should be their concern and not the concern of the state. Many of our states still have laws against all sexual practice, including petting, occurring outside of marriage. These laws should be repealed. No form of sexual behavior should be tolerated that forcibly or deliberately does injury to another person, but no form of sexual behavior should be prohibited that is practiced by consenting adults. We would do well to follow the lead of Albert Ellis, who suggests that ". . . society should not legislate or invoke social sanctions against sex acts performed by individuals who are reasonably competent and well-educated adults; who use no force or duress in the course of their sexual relations; who do not, without the consent of their partners, specifically injure these partners; and who participate in their sex activities privately, out of sight and sound of unwilling observers. If this and only this kind of limitation were applied in modern communities, only a few distinct sex acts would be considered illegal and illegitimate. Included would be seduction of a minor by an adult; rape, sexual assault and murder; and exhibitionism or forms of public display." [16]

THE SOCIAL CONSEQUENCES OF RESPONSIBLE SEXUALITY

Responsible sexuality teaches that the dignity of each individual and of society should be affirmed above all else. Emphasis is thus put on the total relationship. Society has a responsibility both to enhance such relationships of dignity and to respect the rights of individuals who seek their dignity in ways preferred by them, though not condoned by the majority in that society. In this section we shall point to specific areas in which society has a special mandate to develop responsible sexuality.

Sex Education in the Public Schools: There should be compulsory sex education in our public schools, beginning with grade 1 and continuing through grade 12. The current controversy in the United States over sex education is in reality caused not so much by the misguided efforts of the John Birch Society as it is by the sexual hang-ups of many of our middle-aged and older people. Many suggest that parents should teach their own children about sex, which is fine—if it works. But the plain fact of the matter is that many parents do not do this, some of them do it badly, and moreover, sex education is a sensitive subject that is often better taught by the experts. The question today is not whether there should be sex education in the public schools (for who really prefers the back alley?), but, rather, what kind of program should be introduced? Responsible sex education is vital in part because our society has become so sex-saturated. Contemporary movies, literature, art, plays, advertisements—all stress the erotic to such a high degree that a balanced perspective is lost. The churches should accept a crucial role to assist in providing a healthy perspective. However, since their influence is limited and receding, the schools must assume the prime responsibility in many cases. It is unfortunate that many well-meaning citizens in the United States operate on the misguided assumption that sex is dirty and not to be discussed openly. Such an outmoded view only retards the coming of the day when our society will develop a more wholesome and sane attitude toward sexuality.

There is much to be learned from Sweden in terms of sex education. Such education should be introduced into the curriculum as naturally as possible, and become increasingly comprehensive as children progress through the various grades. Instruction should include information on the biological make-up of male and female, the reproductive system of the female, the sex organs, puberty, the facts of menstruation, conception, development of the fetus and pregnancy, masturbation, and the facts of intercourse. This information should be taught in a straight-forward manner, with no facts concealed and with all questions honored. In high school, sex education should include information on the use of contraceptives, abortion, venereal disease, and sexual abnormalities. General agreement exists on what the facts are in these given areas; therefore, there should be no reason why students cannot learn these facts correctly, including the proper terminology. The dangers of contacting venereal disease through promiscuous sexual relationships should be underscored, with venereal disease described as a medical and not a moral problem.

This information should be taught in the context of those values which lead to responsible sexuality, the worth and dignity of each individual, responsibility for the partner, for one's family, and for society. Obviously these values cannot be "preached." They must be shown to make sense in terms of the experiences we can have and should have with our fellow men. Biological facts are not enough; equally important is how these facts influence our interpersonal relationships. If these values do not make sense in sexual encounters, how can we expect them to make sense in all other human confrontations? Sex must be seen as good, wholesome, and properly appreciated within the context of love. Admittedly this is not easy to explain, but it can be done by sensitive teachers.

The crux of the matter is to have such superbly qualified teachers, the point on which Sweden has so seriously erred. Poor teachers can do more harm than good, and therefore it is imperative that these teachers be weeded out and good teachers encouraged in this crucial area. Schools of education and teacher training institutions have a major responsibility in preparing well-qualified personnel. Adult sex education courses should be encouraged not only because most adults need it for their own personal well being, but also because it will help them to communicate more effectively with the younger generation. If the teaching is of high quality and the facts presented in an objective and sympathetic manner, sex education can be eminently successful. Fortunately an organization exists in the United States called SIECUS (Sex Information and Educational Council of the United States), which, under the progressive leadership of Dr. Mary Calderone, has been of inestimable value in developing worthwhile sex education programs. The purpose of SIECUS is: "to establish man's sexuality as a health entity; to identify the special characteristics that distinguish it from, yet relate it to, human reproduction; to dignify it by openness of approach, study, and scientific research designed to lead toward its understanding and its freedom from exploitation; to give leadership to professionals and to society, to the end that human beings may be aided toward responsible use of the sexual faculty and toward assimilation of sex into their individual life patterns as a creative and re-creative force." [17]

Lester Kirkendall, in a pamphlet published for SIECUS, suggests the following guidelines for a successful program of sex education:

1. To provide for the individual an adequate knowledge of his own physical, mental, and emotional maturation processes as related to sex.

2. To eliminate fears and anxieties relative to individual sexual development and adjustments.

3. To develop objective and understanding attitudes toward sex in all of its various manifestations—in the individual and in others.

4. To give the individual insight concerning his relationships to members of both sexes and to help him understand his obligations and responsibilities to others.

5. To provide an appreciation of the positive satisfaction that wholesome human relations can bring in both individual and family living.

6. To build an understanding of the need for the moral values that are essential to provide rational bases for making decisions.

7. To provide enough knowledge about the misuses and aberrations of sex to enable the individual to protect himself against exploitation and against injury to his physical and mental health.

8. To provide an incentive to work for a society in which such evils as prostitution and illegitimacy, archaic sex laws, irrational fears of sex, and sexual exploitation are nonexistent.

9. To provide the understanding and conditioning that will enable each individual to utilize his sexuality effectively and creatively in his several roles, e.g., as spouse, parent, community member, and citizen.[18]

SIECUS has recently received a great deal of unfavorable publicity as a result of right-wing pressure groups whose determination to destroy good programs is surpassed only by their abysmal ignorance. If SIECUS can expand its programs and its influence and be given a fair hearing, then the odds are that the United States will soon have a program of sex education surpassed by no other country. Responsible sexuality stresses the imperative need for such a program.

Birth Control and Abortion: If the primary purpose of responsible sexuality is to promote healthy and loving human relationships, this purpose may or may not include the procreation of children. The traditional approach to sex, we have noted, is for the purpose of procreation. The Roman Catholic Church still upholds this view. But this position is no longer morally compatible with the present population explosion. All evidence indicates that the burgeoning world population is one of man's most critical crises. And the population explosion breeds the horrendous problems of poverty, undernourishment, starvation, and a polluted environment. Man's only hope for sane survival is to cut drastically the growth of population, and this means comprehensive programs of birth control. If such programs do not work on a voluntary basis, then compulsory programs will have to be instituted—programs which could very well involve mass sterilization and euthanasia. In any event, responsible sexuality demands widespread methods of effective birth control. It also means that in most cases procreation is highly undesirable.

Birth control information and devices should be made available to anyone over the age of fifteen who requests them. Of course, there is the danger that some individuals will misuse such information and devices, but this can be true of most anything. A democratic society is committed to the principle that ignorance is more dangerous than information. If we inhibit the free flow of information on the grounds that such information is dangerous, then we should stop pretending that we are a free society, for who determines what is dangerous? In any area of controversy—politics, war policy, religion, sex —the expedient course of action is often to withhold information ostensibly to protect the innocent. The implications of this procedure are too frightening for the open society we claim to be. In a democratic society, one group has no legal right to inflict its moral system upon any other group. Instead, the widest possible latitude must be permitted; and for this reason alone, birth control information and contraceptives should be made available. The impending disaster of increasing world population makes this issue even more crucial, and the dissemination of information even more imperative.

The "pill" has revolutionized methods of birth control with its high degree of effectiveness and minimal chance of error. There are some potentially dangerous side effects to the use of the pill, and every woman should receive proper medical advice before she begins taking such a drug. Medical science hopes that both a "morning after" pill for the woman and a pill for the man will be developed in the near future to make birth control safer and even more effective. One method of birth control which has not been accepted in Sweden but which does seem eminently sensible and practical is voluntary sterilization. For the male this is a relatively simple operation called a vasectomy, which can be performed in a doctor's office and requires virtually no period of convalescence. It is estimated that two million Americans have been voluntarily sterilized, and the number is presently increasing by about 100,000 persons a year, and approximately 75 percent of these individuals are men. A vasectomy in no way interferes with a man's biological functions except to cut off the sperm. It is a myth that a man robbed of his reproductive potential is vulnerable to psychic malaise. This operation should be recommended for all men who wish to beget no more children and perhaps for all men over forty. If men later desire, through remarriage, for example, to become fathers, there are thousands of unwanted children who cry for adoption; moreover, in some cases a vasectomy can be reversed.

Another effective type of birth prevention is abortion. The state laws concerning abortion in this country have been extremely archaic, but fortunately changes are now being made, thanks in large part to the vision of an increasing number of liberal Catholic priests and laymen. Most of the state abortion

laws were written in the nineteenth century, when a desire
for large families in the westward expansion and the lack of
proper medical treatment made abortions highly undesirable.
These laws should be liberalized to make it possible for any
woman to have an abortion for whatever reason she wishes.
The only major restriction should be to prohibit abortion
after the twenty-second week of pregnancy (or when medical
science indicates that the fetus can survive on its own) except
in cases approved by proper medical authorities.

The moral issues involved concerning abortion are extremely complex and critical. How long after fertilization
does "human life" begin? What about the rights of the unborn
child to live? However, all things considered, legalized abortion by consent of the mother seems the best pragmatic answer in a heterogeneous society where the state does not legislate one form of morality. Important, too, is the issue of
women's rights—freedom to have control over one's body.
Some states have recently modified their abortion laws to approve all abortions performed in a licensed hospital by a licensed doctor. We appear to be moving toward a much more
humane attitude on abortion, and this move can only be com-
mended.

Pornography: A further consequence of our modern society
is to repeal all restrictions on pornography. An age limitation
and a ban on public display are to be recommended as are
all the restrictions related to postal laws and international
agreements. The reason for lifting these other restrictions is
that a democratic society has no right to dictate a particular
standard of art and literature for all her members. The most
recent Supreme Court decisions have ruled that to be obscene,
material must appeal primarily to the prurient interest, must
go significantly beyond accepted community standards, and
must be utterly without redeeming social value. By applying
these three tests, the Supreme Court has in recent years ex-

panded the definition of material that is not obscene. As a result, so-called pornographic material now floods the markets, further challenging the interpretation of obscenity.

What constitutes pornography or obscenity is primarily a matter of personal taste, and this is exactly why all adult restrictions on pornography ought to be lifted in the same way that all forms of sexual behavior among consenting adults should be permitted. The three restrictions should concern an arbitrary age limitation such as sixteen, the protection of others from physical injury, and the elimination of public displays. It could very well be that just as the turning point for Denmark came a few years ago when their Supreme Court permitted the showing of *Fanny Hill*, the turning point in the United States could come in the impending court case concerning the Swedish movie *The Language of Love*. It is significant to note that since the Danes removed their restrictions, the sale of pornographic literature has dropped considerably and so has attendance at their world-famed sex fairs. By removing the restrictions, we recognize the legal rights of those persons in a free society who prefer such material. Although extending the limits of art and literature may include material inconsistent with our ideal of responsible sexuality, the determining factor in this case is not our own particular preference, but, rather, the need to protect the rights of the individual members of society. Our society already condones a great deal of practices inconsistent with responsible sexuality, for example, war, discrimination against women, and other forms of violence.

The United States should develop a new standard by which pornography and obscenity can be judged, one that is consistent with our new meaning of the term "promiscuity." Heretofore obscenity has been identified with complete nudity or the use of certain four letter words. Nudity and such words may be in bad taste in certain situations as far as most of society is concerned, but to define obscenity in terms of specific actions, pictures, or words is akin to defining promiscuity entirely in terms of the sex act itself. A more sensible definition of obscenity for our day would be in terms of human relationships, that is, whether actions, pictures and words are in fact degrading to the dignity of an individual or group of persons. For example, the word "nigger" uttered by a white man toward a black man is obscene because its obvious intention is to degrade the black man. On the other hand, the word "shit" is not obscene, but merely in poor taste in that it is used essentially as an expletive uttered in anger or consternation. Similarly the act of sexual intercourse on a movie screen could be beautiful if it shows the fulfillment and intensity of an intimate love relationship between the characters. On the other hand the picture of white men attacking a bus load of black children or a newsreel of soldiers looting a Vietnamese village is blatantly obscene because it is a complete degradation of the dignity of the oppressed victims. Although in a free society none of these pictures should be banned, it would make far more sense, if obscenity is the criterion, not to ban the picture depicting intercourse.

Howard Moody, minister of Judson Church in New York City, has stated well the case for a new definition of obscenity: "For Christians the truly obscene ought not to be slick-paper nudity, nor the vulgarities of dirty old or young literati, nor even 'weird' films showing transvestite orgies or male genitalia. What is obscene is that material, whether sexual or not, that has as its basic motivation and purpose the degradation, debasement and dehumanization of persons. Should we not as Christians raise a new standard of 'obscenity' not obsessed with sex and vulgar language, but defined rather as that material which has as its dominant theme and purpose the debasement and depreciation of human beings—their worth and their dignity?" [19]

The views outlined in this chapter make it appear as though we extoll Swedish standards in sex almost entirely. Indeed, there is little doubt that in our day the Swedish approach to sexuality is preferable to the American way. Sexually, the United States has long been a primitive and backward country. The major difference between the approaches of the two countries is that the Swedes prefer knowledge, openness, and honesty, whereas Americans have sought to promote ignorance, silence, and hypocrisy. The Swedish way is more in keeping with a modern society which tolerates a wide variety of points of view and permits the free exchange of ideas and inquiry. To the degree that the United States is also a modern society, we will need to emulate the Swedish way in enjoyment and acceptance of human sexuality, in sex education, in our understanding of the social consequences of intimate relationships. There is no other way that is compatible with a democratic state. This will be a difficult task, but it is one that we must undertake.

Toward a Theology of Responsible Sexuality

No special theology of responsible sexuality exists any more than one does for the issues of power or race or technology. Theology's role is to relate the teachings of Christianity to these specific areas of human concern. What does the Christian Gospel have to say about the sphere of sexuality? The two major affirmations of the Christian faith are that God is sovereign Love and that God became incarnate in the person of Jesus of Nazareth. Christians believe that the most significant clue to the character of our world at its deepest dimension can be found in the person Jesus, and that this character manifests itself as Holy and Sacrificial Love. When Jesus was asked what one should do to inherit eternal life, he referred his questioner to the Torah: "You shall love the Lord your God with all your heart, and with all your soul, and with all your strength, and with all your mind; and your neighbor as yourself" (Luke 10:27).

The key conviction of Christian faith is that the heart of religion can be found in interpersonal human relationships with the covenant which God has established through Christ with man. The English philosopher John Macmurray has presented a brilliant philosophical justification for religion as relation-centered: "The field of religion is the whole field of common experience organized in relation to the central fact of personal relationship. It is the personal data which are central, and form the focus of attention. Everything is seen, from the religious point of view, in its relation to personality. The personal is the fact of central importance. All other facts are valued in relation to this central value. To put it in simpler if less exact language, the field of religion is the field of personal relations, and the datum from which religious reflection starts is the reciprocity or mutuality of these. Its problem is the problem of communion or community." [20]

It is our conviction that for Christians today Christ must be, above all, the symbol for personal relations. Through Christ we see man in his ideal encounter with other men. What does this mean in practical terms?

It means that only in our human community can we fulfill our own selfhood. Religious language is primarily the language of interpersonal relationships. Our best illustration is the marriage covenant. Why do two individuals wish to be married, ideally speaking? They wish to marry because they sense a power which seeks to bind them into a deeper covenant, a power which makes them want to share their entire lives with each other. The root meaning of the word "religion" is "to be bound." This compulsion cannot just happen, for love has its conditions to be fulfilled. Nor does it usually come with suddenness. Normally it comes only after a period of time in which the two individuals have learned to know each other as *persons* with increasing intensity and intimacy. The marriage ceremony in its symbolism testifies to a new covenant between man and woman to love and cherish each other till death do them part. It is a sacred promise of a new and holy status.

But this love is not automatic, to be turned on and off. Where love is absent in interpersonal contacts, sin is present. Sin is the rupture of the right attitude that can and ought to exist between the two individuals, a rupture which leads to estrangement, anxiety, and insecurity. It means that the covenant is neither whole nor holy, lacking in trust, involvement, and love. A marriage based on selfish intent and not on mutual fulfillment is one in which God is absent. Love, however, is potentially present and can become dominant when its conditions are fulfilled. Through mutual forgiveness and understanding there can occur a confrontation which once again binds the marriage into a new dimension. The marriage can be made "holy and whole"—which is the meaning of salvation. Love is that power which can bind, heal, forgive, and unite persons—that sense of thouness which treats every person, thing, and action as sacred. The enhancement of love is that which each of us craves: to be acknowledged as persons, not as things; to be trusted and accepted. Love, sin, forgiveness, reconciliation, salvation—these are the key terms in interpersonal encounters and in theology as well. We repeat, the field of religion is primarily the field of interpersonal relationships.

Theologically speaking, to believe in God means to acknowledge the height and depth of love in all human contacts. If a man by word and deed shows the supremacy of love in his everyday human experiences, he believes in God. Said Martin Buber, "He who truly goes out to meet the world goes out also to God." [21] Or, as Bishop John Robinson suggests, the real test of one's knowledge of God is "how deeply have you loved?" [22] This is the basic question!

Christ is our model for interpersonal relationships. He puts other people at the center of his life. When we try to explain what the Christian faith means, we point to a person and the quality of his commitments to others. In his excellent book *Living with Sex*, Richard Hettlinger points to the significance of Jesus: "Instead of presenting his followers with another detailed set of regulations, Jesus confronted them with the responsibility of personal decision in the light of the absolute obligation of love—and then assured them that his Father was more interested in the integrity of their response than in the measurement and punishment of their failures. The God of legalism is concerned to keep his hands clean, to uncover evil, and to assign penalties. The God we meet in Jesus Christ runs the risk of association with prostitutes, refuses to condemn a woman taken in adultery, and welcomes us as we are. The reason why many religious people prefer to worship the God of legalism is that they can claim to exercise the divine prerogatives themselves. The follower of Jesus has to accept the more humble role of living as responsibly as he can with the human dilemma, and leaving judgment and forgiveness in the hands of God." [23]

Christ's severest indictment was made against the "religious regulars" of his day, the scribes and Pharisees who should have known better, but who kept substituting externalities for personal witness: "Then said Jesus to the crowds and to his disciples, 'The scribes and Pharisees sit on Moses' seat; so practice and observe whatever they tell you, but not what they do; for they preach but do not practice. . . . Woe to you, scribes and Pharisees, hypocrites! for you traverse sea and land to make a single proselyte, and when he becomes a proselyte, you make him twice as much a child of hell as yourselves. . . . Woe to you, scribes and Pharisees, hypocrites! for you tithe mint and dill and cummin, and have neglected the weightier matters of the law, justice and mercy and faith; these you ought to have done, without neglecting the others' " (Matthew 23:1–3, 15, 23).

The "Seven Great Woes" of the Twenty-third Chapter of Matthew make clear that it is "justice and mercy and faith" which takes priority, and this involves interaction with others. This does not mean that the externals of religion should be neglected, but rather that we must put first things first. Christ shows us that we can be loyal to him only insofar as we, too, center our religious life in our meetings with our fellowmen. He teaches us that although no human life can be free of sin, it is our continuing responsibility to seek at all times to live in a dialogue of love with all our brothers. This is the alpha and the omega of our role as Christians. The acceptance of Christ means the acceptance of every man as his brother and the overcoming of alienation and estrangement. The one who affirms love in his human relationships affirms God. "Beloved, let us love one another; for love is of God, and he who loves is born of God and knows God. He who does not love does not know God; for God is love" (I John 4:7–8).

A theology for responsible sexuality testifies that the new life which is found in Christ will undergird the Christian approach to sex and makes possible encounters based on love. God is at work in and through our relations to others. Sex can never be an end in itself, to be used and abused as a man sees fit. Rather, sex is always an instrument of God's love which seeks to enhance the quality of human interaction.

The Role of the Church for Sexual Responsibility

The role of the church in shaping a responsible sexuality is difficult to articulate for two obvious reasons. On the one hand, there is no one position which the church has ever taken on controversial social issues, since human beings do disagree as to what is right and proper. What one church affirms another church may deny. Indeed, what one group within a particular church affirms, another group within that same church may deny. No church has one spokesman on specific social problems, a fact which is becoming as obvious to Roman Catholicism as it continues to be for Protestantism. Part of this disagreement stems from cultural factors. A "Christianized" African tribe may still practice polygyny. An Italian Protestant community may believe that a woman's place is still in the home. No teachings can be drawn up to cover all specific situations. Jesus recognized this in his refusal to codify his teachings and his continual stress on motivation and the internalizing of the law.

On the other hand, the church and the general society are not one and the same. Not all members of a society belong to any particular church or even to any church. In earlier periods of American history there was a sharp, dogmatic sectarianism which later developed into an implicit pan-Protestant bias. This bias allowed for theological diversity under one vast Protestant umbrella which shaped the country's laws and customs. Today we have become a nation of religious pluralism which respects diversity of opinions for both believer and nonbeliever alike. The church cannot speak for the whole of society. She has the right and duty to express her convictions, but she does not have the right to impose her beliefs and practices on society as a whole; she can influence, but not legislate, public policy.

Keeping these difficulties in mind, what is the proper role for the church in helping to create conditions for responsible sexuality? She must recognize her essential theological mission, which has been so simply and eloquently stated by the late H. Richard Niebuhr: "Is not the result of all these debates and the content of the confessions or commandments of all these authorities this: that no substitute can be found for the definition of the goal of the Church as the increase among men of the love of God and neighbor?" [24]

The whole point of the Christian Gospel is to increase among men the love of God and man through the development of proper human relationships. Christianity affirms that persons are subjects rather than objects and that human beings are more important than things. Christianity teaches that fidelity is more valuable than unfaithfulness, self-respect better than self-degradation, tenderness more human than brutality, love preferable to hate. The Christian ethical principle states that any action or attitude which enhances these values of fidelity, self-respect, tenderness, and love is good, and conversely any action or attitude which undermines them is bad.

The church needs to recognize what the Swedish churches by and large have failed to acknowledge—that in our day it is imperative to develop a reasonable rationale for relating the norm of sacrificial love to sexual behavior. In a society which has become pluralistic, experimental, changing, and relativistic, the church's rationale must address and clarify human sexuality in the light of her understanding of man and contemporary society. This means that for the church there can be no final, absolute, or easy answers to moral ambiguities. Most people are not helped in their understanding and working out of moral dilemmas by an authoritarian ethical code or a dogmatic theological framework that may have worked for their ancestors, who held a radically different world view. It will no longer make sense for a church to insist unilaterally on a particular moral code and then seek to justify the particular code for a pluralistic society.

A case in point is a committee appointed by the British Council of Churches in 1964 to study the problem of premarital sex. This committee was asked to "prepare a Statement of the Christian case for abstinence from sexual intercourse before marriage and faithfulness within marriage, taking full account of responsible criticisms, and to suggest means whereby the Christian position may be effectively presented to the various sections of the community." [25] Thus, the committee was given its conclusions before the study began! For this reason, several individuals who had been invited to serve on the committee refused to do so. The truly amazing fact is that this committee was so thorough and honest in its deliberations that its final report did not condemn sex before or outside of marriage in all circumstances, suggesting instead that "no rule can cover" all possible situations. The British Council of Churches accepted the committee's report as "a valuable discussion" and then proceeded to denounce the report by reaffirming total abstinence outside the marriage covenant. This reaffirmation may have pleased the ecclesiastics who hold the seats of power, but it was clearly irrelevant to the actual situation of the man of today.

There is no hope for reinstating the vanishing moral absolute. The church should not waste her time and resources in such a fruitless task. Her role is to seek a meaningful rationale and viable norms for actions and attitudes and thereby to enhance both for the individual and for society the positive quality of human life. For example, if premarital sex is to be discouraged, then honest studies and experiences must demonstrate that such behavior is, under certain conditions, harmful to the self and to one's relationship with another and that such harm is often not manifested until later in life.

Let us suggest a few norms that the church would do well to uphold as she makes known her mission to the world. These guidelines are relevant for today and consistent with the Christian goal to increase among men the love of God and man. What follows may seem simply to reiterate previously suggested implications of responsible sexuality, but this should not be surprising. The task of the church is not to be unique for her own sake; rather, her task is to join forces with all men of good will who seek responsible sexuality. The true uniqueness of the Christian faith lies in its universality, in its insistence on the supremacy of sacrificial love. The church should welcome the cooperation of all groups and individuals who share a common goal to enhance human relationships and who oppose those who degrade humanity. Thus, insofar as the church serves her members, she also serves society. As Rustum and Della Roy have written in their book *Honest Sex*:

"There are no distinctive patterns of sexual behavior which can be characterized by the absence or the presence of specific acts. . . . The single proper unit by which the Christian measures rightness or wrongness is the absence or presence of concern—of love—for the other." [26]

1. The church should continue to uphold the importance of monogamous marriage. It is a time-tested arrangement that seeks for fidelity, acceptance, and love for the couple and care for young children. Other forms of marriage—polygyny and group marriage, for example—may be appropriate for some individuals under certain conditions. Certainly one-parent families should have no social stigma but become entirely acceptable for our society. For most of us, however, monogamy should remain the ideal arrangement. It is important that the basis of monogamous marriage is redefined to allow for the equal worth of both wife and husband. Each should share the work of the household and each should have similar opportunity to work outside the home if that is desired. Both have as their chief responsibility to be fully human, seeking to develop the talents and opportunities which God has given them. Although some cultures may not yet be ready to take this step toward male and female equality, the church should make this realization her ultimate goal.

The church should also admit that some marriages do not work, that a man and woman can lose their love for one another, and that such marriages should be dissolved. The covenant that is established by the marriage bond should never be taken lightly, neither should it be taken as indissoluble. In a significant number of situations, perhaps an increasing proportion in this unstable world, divorce will be the best solution for all parties concerned. The church should not seek to condemn either party for their failure in marriage, but rather help them to find new meaning to their lives that will lead to a rediscovery of a sense of worth. Compassion is the goal.

2. The church should continue to uphold the importance and even sanctity of the family structure. Every human being needs to belong to a small group, to feel wanted, to be a full-fledged member of a warm and intimate community, and for most people the family can best fulfill this function. But the optimum type of family is not the patriarchal type with the father supreme, the mother running the household, and the children seen but not heard. Today the optimum family structure is one of shared concern in which each individual carries a measure of freedom and responsibility commensurate with his role, age, and experience. It is never easy to find a proper and delicate balance in terms of shared responsibility, but a family that is imbued with love and trust has a good chance of achieving such harmony. In this time when so many dehumanizing factors are at work to undermine the structure of the family, the church must continue to uphold the values of small groups, which are so essential to ensuring the development of stable lives.

Yet the church should also recognize that tensions do develop among fallible persons, that no family can ever be perfect, that at times the strain may prove too much for some of the members. Urbanization, anonymity, and mobility are all unsettling influences on the stability of the family. As more and more functions of the family are transferred to other outside agencies, it is inevitable that family life will become more tenuous and fragile. In this breakdown of family living, the church has the role of seeking to understand and to heal, to find that alternative in living arrangements that will be best for all parties concerned in terms of dignity and self-respect.

3. The church should seek to be sensitive to young people and their sexual desires and how such desires can be creatively controlled. It may be appropriate for the church to make an explicit approval of sexual intercourse for engaged couples, for marriage is in spirit a process which begins with the promise and not with the legal contract. Sexual encounters

between a man and a woman who have pledged their troth to one another can, in times of dreams and romance, become an enriching dimension to a deepening covenant. At the same time the church should uphold the importance of fidelity, that sex is not to be used cheaply or indiscriminately, but in a spirit of tenderness, compassion, and a concern for the consequences. The purpose of sex is to deepen, not to cheapen, the relationship. The church should seek to interpret to young people the beauty of sex but not to condemn those who have abused that beauty. She is an agent of reconciliation and not condemnation.

4. The church should not condemn homosexuality as a disease or perversion from which all men and women need to be saved. The church should indicate a preference for a heterosexual relationship between a man and a woman as best for most individuals in terms of dignity and personal fulfillment. Yet every man and every woman contain both homosexual and heterosexual traits, and which is dominant depends in large part on both heredity and environment—over which the individual has had little or no control. The role of the church is to serve and minister, to make homosexuals full-fledged, productive, dignified members of our society and church with the same rights and privileges as everyone else. The church should also teach that there is nothing inherently wrong in masturbation, that its ethical significance depends upon the use to which it is put.

5. The church should recognize the special situation of the single person who has sexual desires that need to be and should be fulfilled. These individuals should be taught that there is no shame to their indulgence in sex as long as it does not injure the other partner. In the same way the church should discourage extramarital sex, but not condemn indiscriminately each and every individual who may in his extramarital affair have found a satisfactory solution in a particular situation.

6. The church should support programs of sex education in the public schools, churches, and homes. These programs should present values and factual material which give a positive, realistic, and wholesome view of human sexuality. This would include the education of students, teachers, and the community in the exploitation of sex in our culture, and how sex can and should be used as an agent of love and concern. The purpose of sex education should be to utilize sound physiological and psychological information about men and women in a way that will teach the individual how to appreciate sexuality in the context of loving relationships.

7. The church should be a vigorous advocate of all humane forms of birth control. She should have a deep concern for the serious nature of the population explosion and make every effort to teach her people the importance of having small families and the use of contraception. She should encourage widespread programs of education in the desirability of birth control as well as making available birth control devices to every male and female over the age of fifteen. At the same time she should teach her people that the deepest purpose of sex is to enhance the relationship of love and that procreation need not be a necessary goal of the sexual experience. For those married couples who desire children but who are for various reasons unable to have their own, the church should encourage adoption. Adoption should also be a genuine option for single men and women, but proper concern, however, ought to be given to the psychological reasons why the couple or the single person wish to adopt a child.

The church should also seek for the liberalization of laws concerning abortion. Any woman should be allowed to receive an abortion if she wishes, up to a certain point when the fetus is viable. This is a right that should not be abused indiscriminately, and for this reason couples should be taught that effective methods of birth control are always preferable to the abortion of a fetus. Abortions should be used only as a last resort, and the church should recognize and teach that in most cases the tragedy of an unwanted child is far greater than the need for an abortion.

8. The church should favor the removal of all restrictions against obscenity and pornography in literature, movies and the arts, save those restrictions that are needed to protect the innocent and small children. Although she may personally disagree with some of this literature and art, she should be honest and humane enough to encourage diversity in an open society. She should also develop a new concept of obscenity and pornography as having to do with the degradation and dehumanization of a human being. Whatever enhances human dignity is good and whatever degrades humanity is obscene.

The role of the church in developing a responsible sexuality for today is far from easy, and it will never be finished. The church will be damned in whatever she does and damned in whatever she fails to do. She will encounter critics who will regard her as too lenient and permissive, and others who will condemn her as too harsh and regressive. She will agonize and struggle in her continuing search to bring greater meaning and love to a heterogeneous and ofttimes chaotic society. She must be willing to remain open and responsive to new possibilities and patterns that may emerge in man's never-ending search for deeper encounters with his fellowmen.

The concluding reflections of the Committee on Sexuality in the Human Community appointed by the Board of Christian Education of the United Presbyterian Church are worth underscoring: ". . . new technological and cultural dimensions of modern life have provided a radically new spiritual environment in which men and women must understand and use their sexuality . . . as the churches' reflection on these matters has lagged farther and farther behind the new developments, a generation is growing up which takes no notice of what the churches may have said in the past, and looks elsewhere for its understanding of what constitutes mature and healthy perspectives on sex. We think it imperative that the church apply much more flexible and imaginative thought to these problems, since they are so close to the center of one's personal experiences and thus to the sources of one's ethical sensitivities." [27]

The attitude of the church of today toward sexuality must not be couched in negative terms as has been true of the churches of yesterday. "Thou shall not" prohibitions must be replaced by the affirmation "thou shalt love." The positive and wholesome values of sex must be stressed, but at the same time the church should not parrot recent trends in American society and become obsessed with sexuality. This is not her most important area of concern, but rather one issue in a complex set of larger problems involving the human situation: violence, war, poverty, racism, and ecology. If the church could show her greatest compassion for these larger issues and relax her preoccupation with sexual mores, she will probably serve as a more effective agent of reconciliation in all those matters including sexuality.

In the final analysis the church will not be judged by whether she fulfills her mission. Such consummation remains elusive for mortal man. Rather, she will be judged by how faithful she has remained to her primary and prophetic purpose: to seek for the increase among men of the love of God and man. This is her ultimate task in her ministry to the children of God.

AUTHOR'S
NOTES

INTRODUCTION

1. *The New York Times,* May 21, 1970.
2. *The New York Times,* December 30, 1967.
3. *The Oberlin Review,* January 16, 1970.
4. *The New York Times,* April 8, 1970.
5. *The New York Times,* June 1, 1970.
6. *The Holyoke Transcript,* December 8, 1967.

CHAPTER 1: A LOOK AT THE PAST

1. Willystine Goodsell, *Problems of the Family* (New York: Appleton-Century Co., 1928), p. 45.
2. Morton Hunt, *The Natural History of Love* (New York: Alfred A. Knopf, 1959), p. 25.
3. ———, *Ibid.,* p. 26.
4. Y. L. Peretz, *Shalom Bayis* (1889).
5. Charles C. Ryrie, *The Place of Women in the Church* (New York: The Macmillan Co., 1958), p. 89.

6. ———, *Ibid.,* p. 102.

7. ———, *Ibid.,* p. 107.

8. ———, *Ibid.,* p. 111.

9. ———, *Ibid.,* p. 116.

10. Roland H. Bainton, "Christianity and Sex," in Simon Doniger, ed., *Sex and Religion Today* (New York: Association Press, 1953), p. 32.

11. Charles C. Ryrie, *The Place of Women in the Church* (New York: The Macmillan Co., 1958), p. 117.

12. G. Rattray Taylor, *Sex in History* (London: A Panther Book, 1953), p. 153.

13. Willystine Goodsell, *Problems of the Family* (New York: Appleton-Century Co., 1928), p. 65.

14. Morton Hunt, *The Natural History of Love* (New York: Alfred A. Knopf, 1959), p. 110.

15. ———, *Ibid.,* p. 115.

16. ———, *Ibid.,* p. 120.

17. ———, *Ibid.,* pp. 121–122.

18. G. Rattray Taylor, *Sex in History* (London: A Panther Book, 1953), p. 42.

19. Willystine Goodsell, *Problems of the Family* (New York: Appleton-Century Co., 1928), p. 59.

20. ———, *Ibid.,* p. 59.

21. ———, *Ibid.,* p. 63.

22. Vernon J. Bourke, ed., *The Pocket Aquinas* (New York: Washington Square Press, Inc., 1960), p. 220.

23. G. Rattray Taylor, *Sex in History* (London: A Panther Book, 1953), p. 44.

24. ———, *Ibid.,* p. 45.

25. Willystine Goodsell, *Problems of the Family* (New York: Appleton-Century Co., 1928), p. 72.

26. Roland H. Bainton, *What Christianity Says About Sex, Love and Marriage* (New York: Association Press, 1957), pp. 76–77.

27. Willystine Goodsell, *Problems of the Family* (New York: Appleton-Century Co., 1928), p. 78.

28. Morton Hunt, *The Natural History of Love* (New York: Alfred A. Knopf, 1959), p. 223.
29. ———, *Ibid.,* p. 223.
30. ———, *Ibid.,* p. 223.
31. ———, *Ibid.,* p. 223.
32. ———, *Ibid.,* p. 224.
33. ———, *Ibid.,* p. 224.
34. Willystine Goodsell, *Problems of the Family* (New York: Appleton-Century Co., 1928), p. 81.
35. Quoted in Luther's *Table Talk.*
36. ———, *Ibid.*
37. Simone de Beauvoir, *The Second Sex* (New York: Bantam Books, 1949), p. 99.
38. Mary Daly, *The Church and the Second Sex* (New York: Harper & Row, 1968), p. 66.

Other Books Consulted:

Bailey, Derrick S., *The Man-Woman Relation in Christian Thought* (London: Longmans, 1959).

Blenkinsopp, Joseph, *Sexuality and the Christian Tradition* (Dayton: Pflaum Press, 1969).

Burgess, E., and Locke, H., *The Family* (New York: American Book Co., 1945).

Cole, William G., *Sex in Christianity and Psychoanalysis* (New York: Oxford University Press, 1955).

Cole, William G., *Sex and Love in the Bible* (New York: Association Press, 1959).

Lea, Henry C., *History of Sacerdotal Celibacy in the Christian Church* Vols. 1 and 2 (New York: The Macmillan Co., 1907).

Pomerai, Ralph, *Marriage: Past, Present and Future* (New York: Richard R. Smith, 1930).

Stendahl, Krister, *The Bible and the Role of Women* (Philadelphia: Fortress Press, 1966).

White, Sarah P., *A Moral History of Woman* (New York: Doubleday, 1937).

CHAPTER 2: THE AMERICAN WAY

1. Edward N. Saveth, "The Problem of American Family History," *American Quarterly* (Vol. XXI, Summer 1969, No. 2), p. 317.

2. John Demos, *A Little Commonwealth: Family Life in Plymouth Colony* (New York: Oxford University Press, 1970).

3. Edward S. Morgan, *The Puritan Family* (New York: Harper & Row, 1944), p. 7.

4. Arthur W. Calhoun, *A Social History of the American Family* (New York: Barnes & Noble, Inc., Vol. 1, 1945), p. 89.

5. Edward S. Morgan, *The Puritan Family* (New York: Harper & Row, 1944), p. 44.

6. ———, *Ibid.,* p. 29.

7. Arthur W. Calhoun, *A Social History of the American Family* (New York: Barnes & Noble, Inc., Vol. 1, 1945), pp. 58–59.

8. Edward S. Morgan, *The Puritan Family* (New York: Harper & Row, 1944), p. 27.

9. Morton Hunt, *The Natural History of Love* (New York: Alfred A. Knopf, 1959), p. 233.

10. Arthur W. Calhoun, *A Social History of the American Family* (New York: Barnes & Noble, Inc., Vol. 1, 1945), pp. 134–135.

11. ———, *Ibid.,* p. 57.

12. ———, *Ibid.,* p. 58.

13. ———, *Ibid.,* p. 129.

14. Willystine Goodsell, *Problems of the Family* (New York: Appleton-Century Co., 1928), p. 89.

15. Manford H. Kuhn, "American Families Today: Development and Differentiation of Types," in Howard Becker and Reuben Hills, eds., *Family, Marriage and Parenthood* (Boston: D. C. Heath & Co., 1955), p. 134.

16. Arthur W. Calhoun, *A Social History of the American Family* (New York: Barnes & Noble, Inc., Vol. 1, 1945), p. 281.

17. ———, *Ibid.,* p. 245.

18. ———, *Ibid.,* Vol. 2, p. 40.

19. ———, *Ibid.,* p. 46.
20. ———, *Ibid.,* p. 70.
21. ———, *Ibid.,* p. 87.
22. ———, *Ibid.,* p. 90.
23. ———, *Ibid.,* p. 90.
24. A famous saying attributed to Mary Lyon.
25. Robert Fletcher, *History of Oberlin College to the Civil War* (Oberlin: 1943, Vol. 1), p. 373.
26. Quoted under "Women" in *Encyclopedia Americana.*
27. Quoted in Alice Felt Tyler, *Freedom's Ferment* (New York: Harper & Row, 1944), p. 430.
28. Arthur W. Calhoun, *A Social History of the American Family* (New York: Barnes & Noble, Inc., Vol. 2, 1945), p. 119.
29. ———, *Ibid.,* p. 125.
30. William L. O'Neill, *Everyone Was Brave* (Chicago: Quadrangle Books, 1969), p. 17.
31. Arthur W. Calhoun, *A Social History of the American Family* (New York: Barnes & Noble, Inc., Vol. 2), p. 96.
32. ———, *Ibid.,* p. 97.
33. W. F. Ogburn and M. F. Nimkoff, *Technology and the Changing Family* (New York: Houghton Mifflin Co., 1955), pp. 167–168.
34. William L. O'Neill, *Everyone Was Brave* (Chicago: Quadrangle Books, 1969), p. 37.
35. ———, *Ibid.,* p. 40.
36. ———, *Ibid.,* p. 43.
37. ———, *Ibid.,* p. 51.
38. ———, *Ibid.,* p. 56.
39. ———, *Ibid.,* pp. 75–76.
40. ———, *Ibid.,* p. 265.
41. ———, *Ibid.,* p. 303.
42. *Tempo Magazine,* August 1, 1969.
43. ———, *Ibid.*
44. E. W. Burgess and H. J. Locke, *The Family* (New York: American Book Co., 1945), p. 510.
45. *The Atlantic Monthly,* March, 1970, p. 89.
46. Betty Friedan, *The Feminine Mystique* (New York: W. W. Norton & Co., 1963).

47. Morton Hunt, *The Natural History of Love* (New York: Alfred A. Knopf, 1959), p. 337.

48. B. J. Kendall, *Facts for Husband and Wife* (Chicago: Shrewsbury Publishing Co., 1925), p. 50.

Other Books Consulted:

Bell, Robert S., *Premarital Sex in a Changing Society* (Englewood Cliffs: Prentice-Hall, 1966).

Cavan, Ruth S., *The American Family* (New York: Thomas Y. Crowell Co., 1969).

Ditzion, Sidney, *Marriage, Morals and Sex in America* (New York: Bookman Associates, 1953).

Erikson, Kai T., *Wayward Puritans* (New York: John Wiley & Sons, 1966).

Flexner, Eleanor, *Century of Struggle* (Cambridge: Harvard University Press, 1959).

Geiger, H. Kent, *Comparative Perspectives on Marriage and the Family* (Boston: Little, Brown & Co., 1968).

Glick, Paul C., *American Families* (New York: John Wiley & Sons, 1957).

Sirjamaki, John, *The American Family in the Twentieth Century* (Cambridge: Harvard University Press, 1953).

Truxal, A. G., and Merrill, F. E., *The Family in American Culture* (New York: Prentice-Hall, 1947).

Wieman, Regina, *The Modern Family and the Church* (New York: Harper & Brothers, 1937).

CHAPTER 3: SWEDEN AND SEX

1. *Look Magazine,* November 15, 1966, p. 37.

2. Anna-Greta Leijon, *Swedish Women-Swedish Men* (Stockholm: The Swedish Institute, 1968), p. 68.

3. Quoted in Frederic Fleisher, *The New Sweden* (New York: David McKay Co., 1967), p. 237.

4. Anna-Greta Leijon, *Swedish Women-Swedish Men* (Stockholm: The Swedish Institute, 1968), pp. 7–8.

5. Lis Asklund and Torsten Wickbom, *Vägen till Mognad,* 1966, p. 15.

6. Most of these statistics are taken from Hans L. Zetterberg, *Om Sexuallivet i Sverige* (Stockholm: Esselte A B, 1969.)

7. *Handbook on Sex Instruction in Swedish Schools,* 1964, p. 5, 11, 12.

8. Unpublished material.

9. *Handbook on Sex Instruction in Swedish Schools,* pp. 27–28.

10. Birgitta Linner, *Sex and Society in Sweden* (New York: Pantheon Books, 1967), p. 121.

11. ———, *Ibid.,* pp. 113–114.

12. *Handbook on Sex Instruction in Swedish Schools,* pp. 49–51.

13. ———, *Ibid.,* p. 99.

14. Birgitta Linner, *Sex and Society in Sweden* (New York: Pantheon Books, 1967), p. 125–126.

15. *RFSU International Symposium on Sexology,* unpublished report, p. 48.

16. Frederic Fleisher, *The New Sweden* (New York: David McKay Co., 1967), p. 266.

17. Birgitta Linner, *Sex and Society in Sweden* (New York: Pantheon Books, 1967), p. 49.

18. *RFSU International Symposium on Sexology,* p. 148.

19. Unpublished material.

20. Geoffrey Dodd, "Permissive or Promiscuous?" Danish Journal No. 66, p. 5.

21. Leslie S. Hunter, *Scandinavian Churches* (London: Faber & Faber, 1956), p. 17.

22. ———, *Ibid.,* p. 47.

23. Donald S. Connery, *The Scandinavians* (New York: Simon & Schuster, 1966), p. xi.

24. Lars Gustafsson, *The Public Dialogue in Sweden* (Stockholm, 1964), pp. 34–35.

Other Books Consulted:

Ferm, Deane W., "The Role of the Church in Modern Sweden," *The American Scandinavian Review.* Vol. LV, No. 4, December 1967.

Strom, Ingmar, *Kom och Se* (Stockholm: Diakonistyrelsens Bokforlag, 1966).

The Status of Women in Sweden. Report to the United Nations. (Stockholm: The Swedish Institute, 1968).

CHAPTER 4: RESPONSIBLE SEXUALITY

1. Henrik Ibsen, *A Doll's House* (New York City: Dell Publishing Co., 1960).
2. Quoted in Lars Backstrom and Goran Palm, eds., *Sweden Writes* (Stockholm: The Swedish Institute, 1965), p. 227.
3. *The Saturday Evening Post,* April 27, 1963, p. 10.
4. James Gustafson, *The Christian Century,* May 18, 1966, p. 654.
5. Birgitta Linner, *Sex and Society in Sweden* (New York: Pantheon Books, 1967), p. ix.
6. Lester Kirkendall, *Premarital Intercourse and Interpersonal Relationships* (New York: Julian Press, 1961), p. 245.
7. Morton Hunt, *Her Infinite Variety* (New York: Harper & Row, 1962), p. 88.
8. Richard F. Hettlinger, *Living with Sex: The Student's Dilemma* (New York: The Seabury Press, 1966), p. 132.
9. Morton Hunt, *The World of the Formerly Married* (Greenwich: Fawcett Publications, 1966), pp. 233–234.
10. Quoted in Gerhard Neubeck, ed., *Extramarital Relations* (Englewood Cliffs: Prentice-Hall, 1969), p. xii.
11. ———, *Ibid.,* p. 72.
12. ———, *Ibid.,* p. 76.
13. For a good discussion of specific situations, see James A. Pike, *You and the New Morality* (New York: Harper & Row, 1967).

14. Morton Hunt, *Her Infinite Variety* (New York: Harper & Row, 1962), p. 140.

15. Isadore Rubin, *Homosexuality* (SIECUS Study Guide No. 2), p. 7.

16. Albert Ellis, *Sex Without Guilt* (New York: Lyle Stuart, 1958), p. 190.

17. SIECUS Study Guide No. 2, p. 2.

18. Lester Kirkendall, *Sex Education* (SIECUS Study Guide No. 1), pp. 10–11.

19. Quoted in *The New York Times,* January 17, 1965.

20. John Macmurray, *The Structure of Religious Experience* (New Haven: Yale University Press, 1936), p. 23.

21. Martin Buber, *I and Thou* (New York: Charles Scribner's Sons, 1958), p. 95.

22. John Robinson, *Honest to God* (Philadelphia: The Westminster Press, 1963), p. 49.

23. Richard F. Hettlinger, *Living with Sex* (New York: The Seabury Press, 1966), p. 160.

24. H. Richard Niebuhr, *The Purpose of the Church and Its Ministry* (New York: Harper & Row, 1956), p. 31.

25. *Sex and Morality*—A Report Presented to the British Council of Churches (New York: Fortress Press, 1967), p. 5.

26. Rustum and Della Roy, *Honest Sex* (New York: Signet Books, 1968), pp. 191–192.

27. Report of the Committee on Sexuality in The Human Community, Board of Christian Education, United Presbyterian Church, p. 52.

Other Books Consulted:

Atkinson, Ronald, *Sexual Morality* (London: Hutchinson, 1965).

Bailey, Derrick S., *The Mystery of Love and Marriage* (New York: Harper & Brothers, 1952).

Bertocci, Peter A., *The Human Venture in Sex, Love, and Marriage* (New York: Association Press, 1951).

Borowitz, Eugene B., *Choosing a Sex Ethic* (Schocken Books, 1969).

Edwards, John N., ed., *The Family and Change* (New York: Alfred A. Knopf, 1969).

Friedan, Betty, *The Feminine Mystique* (New York: W. W. Norton & Co., 1963).

Greene, Gale, *Sex and the College Girl* (New York: The Dial Press, 1964).

Jones, H. K., *Toward a Christian Understanding of the Homosexual* (New York: Association Press, 1966).

Lilar, Suzanne, *Aspects of Love in Western Society* (New York: McGraw-Hill Book Co., 1965).

Lipton, Lawrence, *The Erotic Revolution* (Los Angeles: Sherbourne Press, 1965).

MacMurray, John, *Persons in Relation* (New York: Harper & Row, 1961).

Masters, W. H., and Johnson, V. E., *Human Sexual Response* (Boston: Little, Brown & Co., 1966).

Mazur, Ronald M., *Commonsense Sex* (Boston: Beacon Press, 1968).

Montagu, Ashley, *Sex, Man and Society* (New York: G. P. Putnam's Sons, 1969).

Myrdal, Alva, and Klein, Viola, *Women's Two Roles* (London: Routledge & Kegan Paul, Ltd., 1956).

Oraison, Marc, *Being Together* (New York: Doubleday & Co., 1970).

Sex and the College Student (Greenwich: Fawcett Publications, 1966).

Sorokin, Pitirim, *The American Sex Revolution* (Boston: Porter Sargent Publisher, 1956).

Winch, Robert, and Goodman, Louis, *Selected Studies in Marriage and the Family* (New York: Holt, Rinehart & Winston, 3rd Ed., 1968).

INDEX

DATE DUE